CHRISTIANS IN CUMBRIA

by John Burgess and others

*Published to commemorate the 850th anniversary of the found…
of the Diocese of Carlisle in 1133*

PREFACE

The Diocese of Carlisle celebrates in 1983 its 850th Anniversary, and major events are being planned throughout the Diocese. There will be special services in all ten Deaneries, some in the open-air in an ancient castle or abbey, some by the lakeside. There are to be exhibitions, competitions, study courses and church trails, with the help of a map published by the Cumbria Tourist Board.

"Christians in Cumbria" has been prepared to show some of the ways in which men and women in this area have tried to follow Christ's teaching through the ages. Its aim is to make us all more aware of our Christian heritage, whether we live in the county or come here as visitors.

The book is to be published on 3rd December, 1982, the day on which the Archbishop of Canterbury will inaugurate the 850th Anniversary celebrations, at a Diocesan Eucharist in Kendal Parish Church.

All profits from the sale of this book will go to the fund set up by the Bishop of Carlisle to provide travel bursaries, to help those coming to this country for training or experience from the Dioceses of Madras and Zululand, linked with the Diocese of Carlisle through Partners in Mission.

ISBN 0 900811 15 3

PRINTED IN ENGLAND BY
TITUS WILSON & SON LTD., KENDAL
1982

CONTENTS

PREFACE AND ACKNOWLEDGEMENTS

INTRODUCTION – by the Bishop of Carlisle

Chapter 1   THE BEGINNING   1-11
The Roman Empire, the Saints of the British Kingdoms,
The Age of Cuthbert, The Viking Threat, Local
Churches of the Post-Viking period.

Chapter 2   THE FOUNDING OF THE DIOCESE OF   12-18
CARLISLE
The First Bishops and their Cathedral, The Chester
Deaneries, Parish Life in the Middle Ages, War and
Disorder.

Chapter 3   THE MONASTERIES   19-27
The Return of the Monks, Why Monks?, Monks in their
Setting, Dissolution.

Chapter 4   EDUCATION IN THE DIOCESE   28-32
The Clergy as Schoolmasters, Education by the
Churches, Growth of State Schools.

Chapter 5   THE WIDER CHURCH   33-38
The Society of Friends, John Wesley and the Methodists,
The other Free Churches.

Chapter 6   THE INDUSTRIAL REVOLUTION AND THE 19TH   39-40
CENTURY IN CUMBRIA
Agriculture and the Enclosures, New Industries, The
Beginning of Tourism, New Challenges to the Churches.

Chapter 7   THE LAKE DISTRICT AND THE DIOCESE   44-46
The coming of the Railways, Wordsworth, Ruskin, The
Keswick Convention.

Chapter 8   THE MINISTRY OF THE PARISH CLERGY   47-50
"Wonderful Walker", The Church and Football, The
Continuity of Worship.

Chapter 9   THE MODERN AGE   51-52

Chapter 10 THE PRESENT AND FUTURE OF THE CARLISLE   53-56
DIOCESE
by Canon David Jenkins. Bricks, Mortar and Money,
Pastoral and Administrative Reform, Synodical
Government, Conference Centres, Partners in Mission,
Clergy and Lay Training.

POSTSCRIPT – by The Bishop of Penrith   57

FINDING OUT MORE – A Book List for Further Reading   58-60

INDEX OF PLACE NAMES   60-62

ACKNOWLEDGEMENTS

The main body of the book has been written by John Burgess of Carlisle, Secretary of the Cumbria Religious History Society, and author of "A History of Cumbrian Methodism". The illustrations are by George Pallant-Sidaway, Lay Reader, of Staveley, near Kendal.

Thanks are due to our two Bishops and to Canon David Jenkins for their contributions, and to many others who have helped. The first three chapters owe much to the hand of John Todd of St. Bees. Deirdre O'Sullivan and Professor Richard Bailey of the University of Newcastle-upon-Tyne have also advised on Chapter 1, and Dr. J. C. Dickinson of Cartmel on Chapters 2 and 3.

There will inevitably be errors and omissions, and these are the responsibility of the 850th Anniversary Committee, and of its Chairman, Spencer Crookenden, who wrote Chapter 8 and also acted as editor, and who will welcome comments and criticisms.

INTRODUCTION

by the Right Reverend David Halsey, Lord Bishop of Carlisle

If you take the old A6 road that leads from Penrith over Shap, you can wander through a score of hamlets and villages, each with its own church. Sometimes the church stands at the centre of the village with the community clustered around; sometimes it is as much as a mile away, showing where once the people lived. But none is likely to be older than the great Saxon tower of Morland Church, built when this area was still in the kingdom of Strathclyde, by some unknown Saxon Christians about a thousand years ago – the only Saxon tower, so it is said, west of the Pennines.

From Morland to Gosforth, from Bewcastle to Barrow, the present Diocese of Carlisle boasts many signs of its great Christian heritage. It is the story of that heritage which this short history aims to tell: how the good news of Christ first came to the north-west: what our Christian forebears were like, what they did and how they laboured to make known to their own generation the good news of Jesus, which they themselves had received.

The Diocese of Carlisle was founded in 1133, but "heritage" is not just an event of the past, it is something which is developed and adapted and is alive in the present. To make the past live does not just mean looking back, it also means seeing how that "past" is active now. So watch the work of reconciliation and unity in action, where three congregations in one of our towns now meet together to worship God and support each other in the task of witness. Visit with me a church set in the centre of the Lake District, where once only a handful of older residents worshipped but where now the worship has come alive with expectation, and where the visitors and the strangers are made to feel welcome and wanted by the fellowship. Or again, there are nearly a score of men and women in training for ministry, and three non-stipendiary ministers – an exciting extension of the full-time ministry – were ordained in 1982. Now in a new way lay people are sharing in the leading of worship and in the pastoral work of parishes, and in many towns and villages the spirit of ecumenism is abroad, and there is a growing commitment among the different churches to each other and to our common mission in Christ. The Radio Officer at B.B.C. Radio Cumbria, who acts for the Church, is an ecumenical appointment supported by all the

Churches. In these ways and in many others, the rich heritage of the Diocese which started 850 years ago is being developed and extended.

It is my hope that this book will make you want to explore and discover for yourself more of what Christians did for Christ in your own area, perhaps 10 years ago, perhaps 1,000 years ago, and then with the help of these pages discover how that story is still being unfolded in the diocese today.

Thanks be to God.

David Carliol

Chapter 1
THE BEGINNING

The Roman Empire

Christ came to Cumbria in the hearts of Romans on the move – merchants, bureaucrats, and possibly soldiers. At Tullie House, Carlisle, you can see the tombstone of a Greek gentleman, Flavius Antigonus Papias, found at Carlisle; and at Brougham Castle there is the tombstone of Titus, found nearby. The language of the inscriptions is believed to show that they were Christians.

This evidence comes from the fourth century, the last century of Roman peace. When the first Christians came to Cumbria, we do not know. Persecuted at some times, tolerated at others, Christian converts spread throughout the Roman empire within a hundred years after the Resurrection. Britain was added to the Empire in 43 A.D. By about 200, Tertullian was writing that "parts of the Britains inaccessible to the Romans were indeed conquered by Christ". By about 304, the British Church recorded its first martyrs. In 313, the Emperor Constantine ordered that "complete toleration should be given by the state to anyone who had given up his mind either to the cult of the Christians or to any other cult which he personally feels best for himself".

Carlisle's key position on the road to Scotland made it the site of an early fortress. Hadrian's Wall was begun in 122 or 123 and from then on Carlisle became a major frontier point, garrison, market and crossroads. It has been surmised that there was a Christian bishop here.

What sort of beliefs had these early British Christians? Just enough comes through to show that the standards they recognised were those we would follow still. Between 420 and 430, Fastidius, a British bishop, addressed a book "on the Christian life" to a devout British widow. He exhorts her not to despise the "rustic bread" he has set before her, for rustic bread can give strength and help to the weary. "The true Christian is he who keeps Christ's command and despises earthly things. Shall he be called Christian who has never fed the hungry, given drink to the thirsty, to whose table no guests are invited, whose roof shelters neither stranger nor pilgrim? Let no Christian think it. That man is a Christian who follows the way of Christ and imitates him in all things."

The Saints of the British Kingdoms

The Roman legions were recalled in 410 from Britain and there followed a gradual breakdown of the Roman civilisation of the towns and the villages. We know very little about this dark period but it would be wrong to assume an immediate collapse into barbarism on the north-west frontier. It was a long way from the pressure of invading Angles, Saxons and Jutes along the east coast. The British tribes of the north had long learnt Roman ways and their leaders became the kings of the successor states in the area.

Analysis of pollens in the Morecambe Bay area and in West Cumbria suggests that there was no decline in agriculture or return of land to scrub until much later. When St. Cuthbert visited Carlisle in 685, he was taken round the walls by a town official of some kind and shown a fountain "wondrously constructed by the Romans" and still in working order. Excavations in Blackfriars Street in 1977-79 showed that the Roman street and building alignment survived into the post-Roman period. It is just possible that Carlisle was one of the very few British towns where some form of settled life continued without a break for the next two or three centuries.

The known leaders of the church in this sub-Roman period were Patrick, Ninian and Kentigern. Cumbria has some claim to connection with each of them; but no connection can yet be proved. Because a church is dedicated to a particular saint, we should not jump to the conclusion that the saint had actually worked in the area. In the absence of independent evidence that a church was in existence in or soon after the saint's lifetime, the dedication may only show the popularity of the saint's cult centuries later.

Thus we would like to think that the place names Aspatria, Patterdale and Preston Patrick show that the founder of the Irish church walked among our hills. We dare not go so far, because these names were formed long after Patrick's period. The teenage Patrick (who died in 461 or 493) had his first sight of Ireland after he had been captured by pirates at "Bannaven Taberniae". This might be Birdoswald (Banna); but there are several contending identifications.

Ninian, who flourished in the first half of the fifth century, established a Christian community at Whithorn across the Solway, and taught the faith to the Picts north of the Forth. The church of Whithorn may have served as a base for the maintenance of the faith on both sides of the Solway. The most likely Cumbrian site associated with Ninian is the remote little church of Ninekirks by Brougham. But although eighth-century metalwork has been found, there is only the shape of the place-name and a tradition of the eighteenth century to show that the church was either founded or dedicated to St. Ninian in the British period. The medieval dedication was to St. Wilfrid.

Kentigern, who probably died in 612, is said to have preached in Strathclyde and in South Wales and to have raised crosses which became the sites of churches. Apart from the bare mention of his death in the Welsh annals, however, the traditions about him are at least three to five hundred years later. There is a notable cluster of churches dedicated to Kentigern in northern Cumbria – Crosthwaite by Keswick, Irthington, Grinsdale, Caldbeck, Castle Sowerby, Mungrisdale, Bromfield and Aspatria. But the dedications may tell us more about the efforts of the bishops of Glasgow to claim northern Cumbria as part of their diocese than about the saint's movements.

"We can never hope for a 'true' picture of early Christian Cumbria" – that was the comment of one scholar who has concentrated for several years on our area. It is to be hoped that archaeological work at Carlisle, on settlements outside Roman forts, on hill forts, and at possible early church sites, will tell us more. So far, there is hardly any evidence of the survival of a British church in Cumbria: a cross-incised slab found at Addingham in 1913, and hints in place-name forms and later historical records. It may be that the Solway basin was one of the areas that kept the faith until the Anglian settlers of the seventh century moved in. It may be that Christianity retreated further west, leaving only a dim memory of holy men and holy places.

The Age of Cuthbert

The British kingdoms yielded gradually to the pressure of Anglo-Saxon invaders from the continent. In the sixth century, the Angles took over the north-eastern kingdoms of Bernicia and Deira (roughly speaking, Northumbria and Yorkshire). By around 650, leaders and some settlers had crossed the Pennines and were controlling the lands of the Solway basin. By the time they are found in Cumbria, they had probably already accepted Christianity. Hardly any pagan Anglo-Saxon burials have been found in the county, and such as have been found are concentrated in the upper Eden Valley.

The Bewcastle cross is the memorial of Anglian Christianity. Even without its head, it stands 14' 6" high looking out over the lonely hills north-east of Carlisle, its carvings nearly as fresh as on the day it was first reared, probably some time after 700. And what carvings! On the west face, Christ stands in classical majesty, one arm raised in blessing, stepping upon the lion and the adder. Above him, is St. John the Baptist; below, St. John the Evangelist. On the

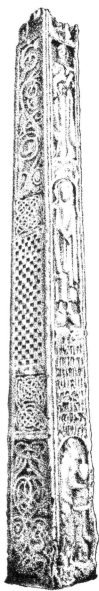

The Bewcastle Cross

east face is a great vine scroll (reminding us of Christ the true vine), inhabited by subtly carved beasts and birds. These carvings are part of the Mediterranean culture, which followed the missionaries from the church of Rome to the Northumbrian kingdom, which then spanned northern England and southern Scotland.

Over into Scotland, in the church at Ruthwell, near Annan, is a cross of similar age in the same style. Sir Nikolaus Pevsner has commented: "There is nothing as perfect as these crosses and of a comparable date in the whole of Europe". The Ruthwell cross has runic writings on it, which help us to get inside the minds of these Northumbrian Christians. They are part of the poem "The Dream of the Rood" in which the Cross itself speaks – a vivid way of teaching the magnitude of Christ's sacrifice. In a more complete, later, version, the poem runs:

"The soldiers on their shoulders bore me,
Until on a hill-top they set me up;
many enemies made me fast there.
Then saw I, marching towards me,
mankind's brave king;
He came to climb upon me.

I dared not break or bend aside
against God's will, though the ground itself
shook at my feet. Fast I stood
who falling could have felled them all.

Almighty God ungirded Him,
eager to mount the gallows,
unafraid in the sight of many
He would set free mankind.
I shook when His arms embraced me
but I durst not bow to the ground,
stoop to earth's surface.
Stand fast I must."

Other Anglian crosses are the earliest evidence of Christian presence at Addingham (Glassonby), Dacre, and Lowther in the Penrith area; at Kirkby Stephen, Kendal, Heversham, and Urswick; and at Waberthwaite, Beckermet, Workington and Brigham in West Cumbria. Some were memorials in churchyards; others may have been erected as a permanent witness and a place where occasional services were held before a church was built. The ordinary Christian of this period would rarely have a local church nearby. He might travel to the services on great festivals at some major church or monastery, such as Carlisle, Dacre, Heversham or possibly Workington. He might hear one of the missionary preachers like St. Cuthbert.

On the backs of the stalls in Carlisle Cathedral, crude paintings (dating from around 1500), show some of the exploits of Cuthbert, who died in 687. Many of the incidents are vouched for by the historian Bede, who lived a generation later, and by another anonymous biographer, and we are on relatively sure ground in telling his story. Ascetic, monk, bishop, preacher, missionary, healer; he was rightly revered in his own day for his integrity, simplicity of life, and spiritual power. He preached the gospel in Cumbria. His welcome by the town officials of Carlisle has already been mentioned, and he is said to have visited a nunnery there in 685, and probably dedicated a church which some would claim to be on the site of the modern St. Cuthbert's. Bede says that he paid annual visits to his friend Herbert, a hermit on an island in Derwentwater, where St. Herbert's Isle commemorates him even now.

After Cuthbert's death, his uncorrupt body soon became the centre of a cult, and the monks who served his church at Lindisfarne regarded him as protector and friend, in death as in life. When the Viking raids finally made life on Lindisfarne intolerable, the monks took up the body of the saint and departed in 875. The exiled monks carried their precious burden and wandered from place to place. They thought of taking it to Ireland – an instance of the continuing links of the Churches across the Irish sea – and actually embarked from the mouth of the Derwent, i.e. Workington. But they were turned back by storm and eventually found a resting place back in the north east at Chester-le-Street. Since the late tenth century, St. Cuthbert's bones have lain at Durham, where today you can see the massive tomb behind the high altar with the one word, "Cuthbertus", upon it.

The Viking Threat

"In the same year (793) the pagans from the northern regions came with a naval force to Britain like stinging hornets and spread on all sides like fearful wolves, robbed, tore and slaughtered not only beasts of burden, sheep and oxen, but even priests and deacons, and companies of monks and nuns." (Anglo-Saxon Chronicle). This was the beginning of the Viking raids which eventually destroyed the monasteries of the north, and came close to destroying the Church itself. First they came to plunder: monasteries were the fairest of all game, especially at times of festival when the treasures of the Church would be on show and people gathered who could be taken as slaves. From about 874 they turned to permanent settlement in the north. At first the pressure was in the east of the country, and the monks of Lindisfarne sought safety in the west. After 900, the Norsemen came across the Irish sea from colonies in Dublin, the

Christ crucified
  from the end of a hogback
  known as the "Saint's Tomb"
  (Church of St. Mary the Virgin,
  Gosforth)

west of Scotland, and the Isle of Man, to settle in Cumbria. Some time between 900 and 925, Tilred, abbot of Heversham, bought estates in Durham so that he might become abbot of Norham-on-Tweed: it reflects the unease of the times, and possibly the end of monasticism at Heversham.

The Scandinavians did not remain pagans for long. As early as 883 the abbot of Carlisle was called in to enthrone Guthfrith as a Christian Danish king of Northumbria. The Scandinavian kings in York normally achieved a working relationship with the archbishops, and some kings were baptised. The settlers in Cumbria were soon made aware of a hero more powerful even than the Norse gods – Jesus Christ.

At Gosforth, the moment of transition from paganism to Christianity is frozen in stone for all times to see. Slender and superbly carved, the Gosforth cross shows on its east face Christ crucified, with the spearman whose lance pierced hs side and a female figure, who may represent Mary Magdalene, a symbol of the converted heathen. This is the only explicitly Christian illustration on the whole cross. The rest of the sculpture, so far as it can be interpreted, is concerned with the story of Ragnarok, the overthrow and destruction of the gods in Norse mythology. Above Christ, for

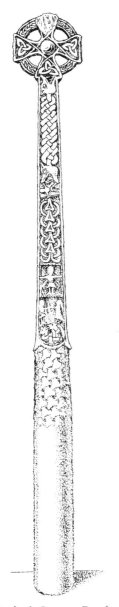

Gosforth Cross — East face

Irton Cross, East Face

Hiberno-Norse Sculpture in Cumbria

SOME OF THE ILLUSTRATIONS in this book depict examples of Viking sculpture belonging to the time when the Irish or Celtic Ch^ch was evangelizing this part of England. We have the famous crosses of Gosforth, Bewcastle & Irton, fragments from other crosses, and hogback gravestones all bearing witness to the manner in which the Word was received by the Northmen of Cumbria.

We are told that when the wise Pope Gregory sent Saint Augustine to minister to the South of England, he gave him instructions not to attempt to destroy & root out those things which the heathen heretofore had held to be sacred, but to convert their holy places to Christian use and to give to their religion its Christian interpretation.

Our Cumbrian carvings shew that the same principle was well understood by the missionaries from Ireland and Scotland. On the Gosforth Cross there is set forth the story of the Ragna Rök, the mutual destruction of the old Teutonic gods and th^r traditional enemies; Good overwhelmed by Evil, but Evil exterminated by Good in what seems a final struggle for the possession of a heaven; heroes set against monsters with the obliteration of both.

Yet Ragna Rök is not the end. Odin, the All-Father, perishes, only to be reincarnated in the person of his son, Vidar, who, through suffering, emerges from the great Dark to open the gate to a New World. The figure on the Gosforth Cross shews how this Triumphant One is identified with the Christ. Heaven is gained; not lost. God survives the holocaust.

instance, there may be Vidarr, taking his revenge against the wolf who slew his father Udinn. Vidarr was one of the gods who would survive the terrible last battle, to rule over a new cleansed world. The sculpture deals with the end of three worlds: the world which Christ redeemed on the cross; the world which would end at his second coming; and the world of the old gods. The parallels and contrasts are deliberately drawn.

The Vikings perhaps posed the strongest threat to Cumbrian Christianity until the rapid social changes of this present century. The Gosforth cross gives us a hint as to how the threat was met. The existing beliefs of the newcomers were fitted into a Christian framework: the method is still valid in a missionary situation today. St. Bega's ring is another instance. It was common among the Vikings to swear solemn oaths upon a "ring of power" – so King Alfred's treaty with the Danish leaders was ratified in 876. At St. Bees, from the twelfth century to sixteenth, the Benedictine monks were guardians of just such a ring, still being used to establish the truth of legal evidence. By then the monks believed that the ring had belonged to a local saint, Bega – a virgin from Ireland who had refused to be married off to a Scandinavian prince. She fled, sailing singlehanded to land at St. Bees. Whether this is based on fact or not, the practice of swearing upon the ring was almost certainly started in a pagan context and was sanctified by the church.

Local churches of the post-Viking period

The Anglian kingdom of Northumbria dwindled away before the Vikings. The Scandinavian kingdom of York was short-lived. While most of the rest of the country was unified under the kings of the line of Wessex, Cumbria – or northern Cumbria at any rate – for much of the tenth and eleventh centuries formed part of the Scottish kingdom of Strathclyde. By now the language and culture of the area was a remarkable mixture of British, Norse and Anglian elements.

At Morland, where the fine eleventh century west tower survives, we can at last catch a glimpse of the life of Christians in a local church. It must have seemed a lavishly built church when it was new, for stone building was rare. Churches of wood, or wattle-and-daub, were commoner, like the little chapel of Triermain, near Lanercost in Gilsland, which was constructed of logs or poles in the time of Bishop Aethelwine of Durham (1056-71).

There were still few parishes as we know them. A rich landowner might establish a church to serve his own estate: for the rest, large areas probably came under "minster" churches, served by groups of priests. The places which received the name Kirkby, "church settlement", from Norse speakers, may have had such minsters – Kirkby Lonsdale, Kirkby Stephen, Kendal (once Kirkby Kendal), Kirkby-in-Furness, and St. Bees (formerly Kirkby Beghoc). At Cross Canonby and Dearham, Lowther and Walton, Brigham and Dacre, at Kendal and elsewhere the twisted scrolls and plaits, the twining, biting beasts of the Anglo-Scandinavian style of carving, identify the churches that were already in being when the Normans came.

Morland Church, by J. Ashworth

Entrance to Aspatria Church, from a print of 1814

Chapter 2
THE FOUNDING OF THE DIOCESE OF CARLISLE

The First Bishops and their Cathedral

On 6th August, 1133 the first Bishop of Carlisle was consecrated by Archbishop Thurstan in York Minster. His name was Athelwold (Aethelulf or Adululf are variants) and he was Prior of the Augustinian canons of Nostell near Wakefield. He had also acted as King Henry I's confessor, an instance of the King's "strange and somewhat contradictory personal taste for northern Anglo-Saxons" (Kapelle). By personal taste or statesmanlike conciliation, it was an Anglian cleric whom the King chose to lead the church in the last part of England to be added to the Norman realm.

We think of 1066 as the date when the Normans conquered England. But when Domesday Book was compiled in 1086, the royal agents looked no further north than Bootle in the west of Cumbria and Kendal in the east. The rest was either Scottish or lawless. In 1092, King William II captured Carlisle, and over the next twenty or thirty years castles were built, and Cumbria parcelled out among the King's barons, mainly Normans, but with a sprinkling of native English.

The new diocese was established to ensure that church government on the frontier was in the hands of a man whom the King knew and trusted. It was also to stem the claims of the bishops of Glasgow, one of whom as late as 1267 was still claiming that the southern boundary of his diocese should be on Stainmore. But the job was only half done. The see was tiny, the area poor and disorderly, and far from the seats of power. The bishopric was under-endowed, and when Athelwold died in 1157 no successor was appointed. There was an abortive attempt to find a bishop in 1186. "Ultimately in 1203, perhaps in a fit of perverse humour, King John gave to the bishopric a vagrant bishop of Ragusa who is unlikely to have regarded Cumbria as a home from home" (J. C. Dickinson). Thereafter the succession was better kept.

Athelwold was both a religious and political ruler, acting as King Stephen's ambassador in 1138 in negotiations with the Scots, and then coming to terms with new rulers. For the Scots, King David took advantage of civil war in England to re-assert the Scottish claim to north Lancashire, Cumbria, Northumberland and Durham, which the Scots held to 1157. Carlisle was one of David's favourite residences; here the future King Henry II of England was knighted by him, and here David died.

So the rulers of both England and Scotland probably had a hand in the construction of the first cathedral. A house of Augustinian canons was established in 1122/3 and their church was under construction in 1130. In 1133, the church became the cathedral and the canons its staff.

Today just the massive arches of the transepts and two bays of the nave survive to remind us of the beginnings of the diocese. Fire destroyed the twelfth-century chancel, and it was gradually replaced in a lighter, more graceful style, culminating in the superb east window of c. 1350 – in all, the finest Christian monument in the Diocese. Six bays of the nave were pulled down in the 1640's and never replaced.

The Chester Deaneries

The boundary of the medieval diocese cut across Cumbria, went inland up the Derwent, along the watersheds by Dunmail Raise and took in the northern half of Westmorland. The rest remained part of the archdeaconry of Richmond in the archdiocese of York, until 1541, when it was transferred to the bishopric of Chester. Only in 1856 did the diocese take its present shape, almost coterminous with the civil county of 1974 (this book deals with the larger area at all periods).

The Richmond deaneries were in double isolation – separated by the Pennines from their archdeacon, and by their archdeacon from the Archbishop of York. For most of the middle ages the Archdeacon of Richmond had virtually all the rights of a diocesan bishop, save only those of consecrating churches and ordaining clergy. Only when the archdeaconry was vacant, or by special arrangement, could the archbishop exercise his right of visitation, i.e. touring the parishes and enquiring into the discipline of the clergy and the morals of their congregations. William Melton, a conscientious and effective archbishop (1316-1340) conducted only three or four visitations of the archdeaconry in 24 years, and only once did he cross the Pennines in person. We can trace his progress in October 1331 from one little gathering of clergy and laity to another – Cartmel on the 17th, Conishead and Dalton on the 19th, Whitbeck (21st), Ponsonby (22nd), Egremont (23rd) and an unnamed place (Workington or Dean perhaps) on the 24th, before beating the winter weather back to York. What he found is not recorded.

Parish Life in the Middle Ages

At Bolton near Appleby, two carved knights on horseback fight on: they could almost have ridden off the Bayeux tapestry. All over

The Two Knights, Bolton Church, near Appleby

Cumbria, their colleagues, the new Norman landowners, were using the surplus wealth that came from conquest and an expanding economy to re-build existing churches in stone and set up new ones. In the nave at Kirkby Lonsdale (inspired directly by the then new Durham cathedral) and in the parish church at Torpenhow, we get some idea of the setting of twelfth century worship.

The style is what we now call Romanesque, because those who used it all over Europe were looking back to a supposed Roman past. It is marked by heavy pillars and rounded arches, deliberate patterns of zig-zags, nail-heads, and beak-heads. Here in Cumbria, some of the fantastic vigour of the best Scandinavian work seems to live on as well. There are exuberant interlace carvings on a lintel at St. Bees, strange heads of men and beasts in the chancel arches at Torpenhow and Gosforth, and dragons over a door at Long Marton and on the font at Bridekirk. It is individual work – the Bridekirk font is signed "Rikarth made me" and there is a little self-portrait of the sculptor hammering away.

Gradually more refined good manners of the Early English style, with pointed lancets, took over. Cumbria is not rich in surviving instances in its parish churches, although there are Early English features at Scaleby, Castle Sowerby, and Clifton. The monastic churches at Lanercost, Calder, St. Bees and Shap were all brought to completion in the thirteenth century. No sculptor signed the lovely statue of St. Mary Magdalene who still looks down, her lips half smiling, from the top of the west front of Lanercost Priory.

St. Mary Magdalen,
Lanercost Priory

G.E. Pallant-Sidaway '82

The architecture of the Norman period fuses continental influences with hints of a Viking past. Henry I found places for members of native families in the bishopric and in secular lordships. While some of the churchmen of Cumbria organised the church into deaneries and parishes, held synods and legislated in true Norman style, others were re-affirming the ancient local roots of the Faith. A monk of Furness Abbey called Jocelyn wrote a life of St. Kentigern. An anonymous author, lamenting that the life of St. Bega was but scantily recorded, hastened to fill the gap, claiming to draw upon "chronicles and authentic histories, and the verbal accounts of truthful men". Despite conquest – perhaps because of it – the continuity of Christianity was important.

The builders of the new churches were not always content to let them remain chapels of some remote mother church, and the vast parishes of the pre-Norman period were subdivided. An inquest in 1185 found that one Copsi (another non-Norman landowner) was the "lord and founder" of the church of Corney (near Bootle) between 1147 and 1153 – another parish carved out of St. Bees. The beginning of Burgh-by-Sands as a parish is also recorded about this time. But as late as 1444 or 1445, the inhabitants of the chapelry of Eskdale were petitioning the Pope for parochial rights. They said they were ten miles away from the mother church of St. Bees (in fact, more) and separated from it by two broad stretches of water and three streams which swelled in rainy and wintry weather, so that the parishioners could not conveniently go to St. Bees for christenings, burials, divine offices, sacraments and sacramentals. The petition was not wholly successful: Eskdale may have obtained burial rights, but was still part of the parish of St. Bees until the nineteenth century.

What did Cumbrians think about when they sat or stood (for seats were few) in church while the priest spoke the Latin, which none save he would understand? We shall never know in detail: neither wall-paintings, nor much stained glass, nor local sermons, have come down to us. No doubt they thought more about death and judgment than we do, and hints of medieval Christian teaching come down to us in wills, written usually by the parish priest in the name of the testator, and at his deathbed. "I, John son of Roger, lately from Lancaster, of sound mind and good memory, make my will as follows. First I give and bequeath my soul to God who created it out of nothing and redeemed it with His own blood, and to the blessed Virgin Mary and all saints, and my body to be buried in the chapel of St. Cuthbert of Milburn" (Will of 1354). There was growing concern that one's memory should be preserved on earth after death, and that prayers should be said to speed the passage of one's soul through purgatory to heaven – if one could afford to pay for them. So at Cartmel Priory is the fine tomb of Sir John of Harrington who died in 1347. At St. Bees the body of a layman has recently been found, almost perfectly preserved by being wrapped in a shroud, coated with resin or tar, with an outer wrapper of lead sheet. Wills called for prayers on the anniversary of death or for a period after it, and the well-to-do established chantries, with a priest paid to pray daily for the soul of the founder. One of the earliest chantries was endowered in a new chapel at Bramwra in 1300 (later transferred to Hutton-in-the-Forest). The last was founded in Kendal Parish Church, apparently in 1543, long after the fashion for them had died further south.

Our notional parishioner might well have been thinking, not about death, but about the week's dinners. The parish church was almost too much the meeting point of the community, and one of the recurrent concerns of the bishops of Carlisle was to stop markets in churchyards. In 1306, the people of Cockermouth complained that the congregation of Crosthwaite bought and sold in their churchyard every Sunday, corn, flour, peas, linen, cloth, meat, fish and other merchandise (to the detriment of Cockermouth market). A fourteenth century decree of the diocesan synod forbade public markets and pleas (court hearings) to be held in churches, porches or churchyards on Sundays or other days – and also banned "lewd dances" or other shameful plays on festivals of the church.

War and Disorder

Edward I's intermeddling in the affairs of Scotland after the death of King Alexander III in 1286 brought an end to more than a century of almost uninterrupted peace on the northern border. Invasion was repaid with invasion, raid with raid, plunder with plunder, and Cumbria suffered. The peel towers that were erected all over the county in the next two hundred and fifty years tell of the resources that had to be directed to safeguard men and cattle against intermittent border warfare.

Few churches were built or re-built in these years. Some that were built resemble fortresses themselves. The tower of Newton Arlosh (after 1305) is a peel tower, with doorway at first floor level, and the ground floor tunnel-vaulted for added strength. Burgh-by-Sands and Great Salkeld towers are similar. Even more remarkable is the church at Boltongate (c. 1500), just off the Carlisle-Cockermouth road, where the whole roof of the nave is a stone tunnel rising in a pointed vault. Yet the chancel of Carlisle cathedral shows that men

were on occasion still able to spend lavishly to the glory of God, and the merchants of Kendal, Appleby and Kirkby Lonsdale were prospering sufficiently to pay for extensions to their parish churches in the "perpendicular" style.

It is a reminder of the dangers of Cumbria that the bishops of Carlisle lived, and still live, not in a palace, but in a castle. Early bishops lived in the Augustinian priory at Carlisle, and had strongholds at Linstock and Bewley in Bolton parish. But from the thirteenth century, Rose Castle has been their main residence – chosen because it was on the safer side of Carlisle, with the town between it and the Scots, and handy for the road south. The name itself tells of the pleasure which the bishops found in this retreat. The fortifications were strengthened and re-built by Bishop Kirkby after 1346. Bishop Kite (1521-1537) gave Rose a fine new gateway in the early days of the Tudors. The castle was severely damaged in the English civil wars; the south and east wings were pulled down by Edward Rainbowe (1664-1684). Finally, Bishop Percy expended large sums making the place fit for a grandson of the duke of Northumberland (1827-1856).

The medieval bishops did not always get a good press, especially when asking for money. Around 1281 a witty monk of Lanercost commiserated with his bishop's flock:

> "Poor sheep, with cares already worn,
> You should be comforted, not shorn".

But much was expected of the bishops. By turns they were pastors, administrators, diplomats and generals, sometimes even borough surveyors – for Ralph Ireton (1218-1292) was commissioned to see to the cleansing of the streets of Carlisle, and William Strickland (1399-1419) gave Penrith a public water supply. Ireton also helped to negotiate the marriage of Margaret, Alexander III's short-lived heiress of the throne of Scotland, to Edward I's son. Several bishops are found acting as custodians of Carlisle castle, and commissioners for the negotiation of truces and peace on the Scottish borders in the fourteenth and fifteenth centuries. Most warlike of them all was John Kirkby (1332-1352), who helped to relieve the siege of Edinburgh in 1337, routed a Scottish raid on Cumbria in 1345, and commanded a wing of the English army at the Battle of Neville's Cross in 1346.

Chapter 3
THE MONASTERIES

The Return of the Monks

In 1073 a little group of monks set out from the Cotswolds for the north of England, their vestments and books on the back of a donkey. They had read their Bede. One of them had seen the ruins of Whitby. They knew about the great Northumbrian monasteries of Jarrow and Monkwearmouth. They knew too that the Vikings had ended it all. These monks went out as pilgrims but they stayed as the founding fathers of a monastic revival which spread rapidly throughout the north. In 1088-9 monks from the new Whitby established St. Mary's Abbey, close to York Minster: St. Mary's in turn sent out colonies, to Wetheral between 1106 and 1112, and to St. Bees between 1120 and 1135.

These men were Benedictines, following the rule laid down by St. Benedict in the sixth century – the same rule, presumably, as was followed in the vanished Anglian houses at Carlisle, Dacre and Heversham. Close behind came representatives of another order following, in practice, a very similar way of life, the canons regular of St. Augustine. This order grew in popularity after King Henry I had founded Holy Trinity, Aldgate in 1107-8. It was Henry I again who brought canons from Nostell near Wakefield to Carlisle, probably in 1122-3, with a view to their staffing the projected new cathedral. In contrast to that busy town site, the next Cumbrian canons went from Pentney in Norfolk to settle in an isolated valley up in Gilsland, at Lanercost, between 1165 and 1169. Between 1189 and 1194, canons from Bradenstoke in Wiltshire came to Cartmel; and before 1181 Conishead was converted from a hospital to an Augustinian priory.

Early in the twelfth century, a new wave of monasticism fired men's imaginations, especially in the north of England. It was an austere way, a hard way; rejecting all kinds of luxury, seeking the remotest sites, tilling the land with the labour of the communities themselves (especially lay brothers); simplifying the liturgy to allow more time for reading, manual work, and private prayer. The movement started at Cîteaux in Burgundy in 1098. But the first of the stricter houses in Cumbria was not Cistercian but Savigniac, belonging to an order with similar ideals, which united with the Cistercians in 1147. Monks from Savigny came to Tulketh in

Lancashire in 1124, and moved to Furness three years later. Furness in turn sent a colony to Calder in 1135, and after they fled before a Scots raid (in 1138) a second colony was sent out in 1142 or 1143. While Cumbria was part of Scotland at the end of 1150, Henry, son of King David I, brought Cistercians from Melrose to Holm Cultram. There was a reform movement among the canons also, and stricter "Premonstratensian" canons from Cockersand came to Preston Patrick, near Kendal, around 1190, and moved to a remoter site at Shap roughly ten years later.

Women in Cumbria had little opportunity for the religious life. There were two tiny nunneries, both Benedictine, one known as Armathwaite and situated at Nunnery near Kirkoswald, and the other at Seaton near Bootle. They were founded before 1200 and 1210 respectively.

After Cistercianism came the most radical religious movement of all – the friars. Rejecting all land endowments, they aimed to beg their bread from day to day and to live as true disciples of Christ. They did not retreat from the world, but settled very largely in towns, preaching and hearing confessions. Each of the main orders was represented in Cumbria by one house – Dominicans and Franciscans in Carlisle, Carmelites at Appleby, and Austin Friars at Penrith.

This completes the tally of the houses of the monastic and mendicant orders in the county. But there are many more places associated with them. They were given parish churches as their endowment – for instance St. Mary's, York, had the patronage of Kirkby Lonsdale and Kirkby Stephen parishes from the beginning of the twelfth century. They were given lands far from the house itself, which meant setting up centres of estate management known as granges, usually under bailiffs or lay brothers. Thus Furness Abbey had a grange at Hawkshead, and another in Borrowdale (as the name Grange-in-Borrowdale still recalls), while the Gilbertines of Watton had a grange or cell at Ravenstonedale. There were also a number of quasi-monastic foundations known as "hospitals", for the relief of the poor, the elderly, the sick, or travellers, at various times in the middle ages – at Bewcastle (1294), Carlisle (three: 1199-1645, 1246-c. 1350, and 16th century), Holm Cultram (16th century), Wigton (1383-1546), Caldbeck (1170), Gilswath-in-Bampton (c. 1290), Appleby (1240-1544), Sandford near Warcop (1265), Brough (1506), Ravenglass (c. 1180), Scalthwaiterigg near Kendal (12th century to 1536), Furness (13th century to 1537), and Kirkby Lonsdale (16th century).

Why Monks?

What impelled Henry I, or William le Meschin, Lord of Copeland, or Robert de Vaux, Lord of Gilsland, to give up land and revenues to a monastic house? What brought the monks and nuns themselves into the regulated life of the cloister? It is tempting today to account for the monks in the terms we ourselves find easiest to understand. For the lay founder, his priory or abbey was a fashionable form of conspicuous display, like the modern industrial baron endowing a university college. It was relatively easy to be generous with the proceeds of recent conquest. It was also a spiritual insurance policy, for the good of the souls of the founder, his ancestors and successors, as so many charters state. It was a way of obtaining the improvement of marginal lands, pasturing the valleys of Eden and Calder and Derwent, clearing the forests of Gilsland or draining the marsh-ringed levels of the Holm. For the monks, it was a life of good works – the entertainment of travellers (Cartmel and Conishead were responsible for providing guides and beacons for travellers across the sands of Morecambe Bay); the feeding of the poor (the canons of Cartmel in 1535 gave 11% of their income in alms, spending £12 on daily gifts to seven poor men); the education of the tenants'' sons (as we know happened at Furness). It meant also a life of security and established social status, a life for many talents – estate management, building, writing, preaching, church and national administration (abbots of Holm Cultram, for example, were twice in charge of the see of Carlisle in vacancies, and attended parliaments between 1294 and 1312: another aspired to be bishop himself, and ambition drove him mad).

All this is true enough, but we must also judge the monks on their own terms. Nothing we have said so far is sufficient to account for the esteem given to monks and canons, especially in the twelfth century, and to friars in the thirteenth. That esteem was not based on any kind of end-product that our modern times can easily recognise: it was simply that the religious orders were closer to God. The friars were valued for their evangelism, their good works, their poverty; the monks and canons for their constant round of prayer and psalmody, which took from 4½ to 6 hours each day. The ideals of the orders could, and did, slip into empty formal routine; but they never wholly lost sight of their main purpose, which was to serve God worthily in a life of discipline, charity and peace, freed from the pressures of a doomed and disorderly world.

Monks in Their Setting

Even in ruins, the monks' buildings are among the most evocative remains of the middle ages. At Furness, for instance, you can see a section of the precinct wall that marked the boundary between the

self-contained world of the Abbey and that outside. The precinct was entered by a gatehouse -- the Rule of St. Benedict advised that it should be kept by a "wise old man, who understands how to give and receive a message and whose years will keep him from leaving his post". Gatehouses in Cumbria survive at Wetheral, Cartmel and Calder (the last is on private ground). To understand the layout inside the precinct, go to Shap, where there is a complete ground plan. The heart of the monastery was the church – and you can worship today in Carlisle cathedral, at Holm Cultram, St. Bees and Lanercost, between walls that once echoed the singing of monks or canons regular. Usually to the south of the church lay the cloister, the walkways being used also as workrooms. Along part of the east side of the cloister was the chapter house, where the daily business meeting of the community was held, and above this was the dormitory – there are good examples at Furness and Calder. On the opposite side of the cloister to the church was the fratry or refectory – Carlisle, much restored, is the best Cumbrian example. The west range was used in Cistercian houses for lay brothers, and in other orders for guesthouses or lodgings for abbot or prior. At Lanercost, part of the west range is still in use as a parish room, but this was much altered to make a house for Sir Thomas Dacre after the canons left.

A lot is known about the routine life that went on within such walls, but the evidence comes from outside the county, and must be sought in general books on the monastic life mentioned at the end of this book. Between 1298 and 1316, however, the little-known Chronicle of St. Mary's Abbey, York, carries entries about St. Bees, which lift time's curtain on a few of the things which the monks themselves found memorable.

In 1298, Nicholas of Saddington died suddenly at St. Bees on Christmas Day, at the hour of matins – a sentence that calls up an impression of the dark church beset by winter's cold, the consternation of the little community of seven or eight monks as their brother collapses during the long midnight office. "He was the best reader of the gospel": that was the chronicler's obituary. On 5th June 1308, Stephen of Gilling became Prior, and two days later the Chapel of St. Bega (it is not clear whether this means the whole or part of the church) was placed under interdict for the shedding of blood. Worship was suspended for a year, until with great ceremony lasting two days the Bishop of Carlisle and Prior of Wetheral came down to lift the ban. Shortly after, there is another glimpse of monastic ceremonial on the grand scale: "a general decree was made regarding the liberties of St. Bees by eight monks and priests vested

West front of Lanercost Priory, from a print of 1814

in albs and maniples, with candles burning and before the relics; in token of which the finger of St. Bridget the Virgin (*viz.* a statue) oozed oil". The cult of the local saint Bega was active in those years: "in 1310 God worked many miracles by the prayers and merits of St. Bega – giving speech to the dumb, sanity to the demented, purging to the dropsical, with many seeing and hearing". In 1311, there is a reminder of the close relationship between monks and local landowners: "John of Pardshaw died, who was steward for almost twenty years . . . a just man and always of good will". (As steward, John would hold court sessions for the monks and advise on management of the estates.) Another landowner in 1312 did homage to the Prior of St. Bees in the presence of all the brethren for land at Arlecdon – the context suggests that he was eating humble pie at the conclusion of a longstanding dispute. Under Stephen of Gilling, the monks of St. Bees were active in promoting the cults of the saints they served, active in asserting their rights and liberties. But in 1315 came a disaster: the Scots raided West Cumbria "and carried off to Scotland the draught animals and all the ecclesiastical vestments (of the Priory) . . . They slew the men resisting them, because they lacked a leader". For Stephen of Gilling, it must have been a bitter blow. He was dead within fifteen months and was buried in the church.

Powerful landowners in an age of expanding agriculture, the monks of the twelfth and thirteenth centuries left their mark upon the landscape far beyond their precincts. Once again, Shap is a good starting point. Alongside the modern approach lane you can still see the medieval approach road to the original bridge, and farm track-ways hollowed by medieval traffic. Out to the west, ancient dykes still show the limits of where their men cut a livelihood from the fellsides.

Farther north beside the Solway, four miles to the north-east and eight miles to the south-west of Abbey Town, the farmlands are probably the creation of the Cistercians of Holm Cultram, who drained the marshes, saw to the making of sea defences, and created a landscape almost without villages. The exception is Newton Arlosh, deliberately founded as a new town about 1304, after the monks" borough at Skinburness was destroyed by the sea.

At St. Bees it is possible to trace for nearly a mile the channel by which, around 1250, water was brought out of the Rottington valley, round a ridge, to turn the Priory's millwheel in the valley of the sluggish Pow Beck – no small feat of surveying and construction. The bareness of the fellsides of central Lakeland may be due partly to the grazing of monastic flocks, and in upper Eskdale you can still

The Monastery of St. Bees, from a print of 1775

see the remains of the boundary walls constructed for the monks of Furness around part of their 14,000 acre estate at Brotherilkeld soon after 1280.

Dissolution

In 1530 the Cumbrian monasteries seemed set in their quiet ways. There were probably around 160 monks, canons and nuns (no estimate for friars is possible) compared with 100 in 1379/81, when the plague had severely reduced numbers. Some houses were enriching their buildings – Furness was building a fine west tower; Shap did likewise after 1500, and Abbot Chambers added a new west porch to Holm Cultram in 1507. Some were still enriching their spiritual life, although there were scandals. Gavin Borrowdale, a monk of Holm Cultram, was suspected of poisoning his Abbot in 1532. Alexander Banke, Abbot of Furness from 1509 to 1531, was at odds with tenants and neighbours, and "under his rule the Abbey was operated as a property company rather than a religious house" (Haigh). People were questioning whether the monks still justified their privileged position; and some were suggesting that their wealth would be better employed in the hands of King Henry VIII.

So in the spring of 1536 an Act was passed dissolving all English monasteries with a net annual value of less than £200. The year

before, commissioners had made a rapid valuation of monastic wealth; and the King had sent his visitors to gather scandal about the lives of the religious. (The visitors for the north-west were probably Cumbrians – Dr. Richard Layton of Dalemain, and Dr. Thomas Legh whose brother had land in Frizington.) The Act of 1536 suppressed Cartmel and Conishead, Seaton and Calder, Armathwaite and Lanercost, and the king's commissioners confiscated their property.

Shap Abbey, from a print of 1812

There was a swift popular reaction in the winter of 1536/7. In some parts of the country the rising known as the Pilgrimage of Grace was due to agrarian discontent, but in the north-west the dissolution was the cause. The rebels expressed the shock of the northern countryside at the ending of a stable and familiar way of life, and the loss of charitable and spiritual services which were still valued. The abbots of the major houses of Holm Cultram and Furness gave support to the rising; and for a time the rebels restored the canons to Cartmel and Conishead, the nuns to Seaton and the monks to Calder.

When peace had been restored, the royal commissioners descended upon Furness, and the Abbot and monks set in train the second phase of dissolution by "voluntarily" surrendering their house to the Crown in 1537. Holm Cultram followed within a year. Wetheral went in 1538, St. Bees in 1539, Shap (reprieved in 1536, possibly because of the hospitality it gave to travellers) and Carlisle were surrendered in 1540. By the end of that year, there were no monasteries left in England.

There were jobs for some of the religious under the new order. The last Prior and some of the canons of Carlisle became the Dean and Chapter of the re-founded cathedral in 1541. Gavin Borrowdale, last Abbot of Holm Cultram, became the first vicar of the parish with a princely income. For others there were more or less adequate pensions. For all the friars, and some monks and canons from the 1536 dissolution, there was nothing but permission to take a secular priest's job if they could get one. For four canons of Cartmel, unwise enough to take up arms to save the old ways, there was only the hangman's rope.

Only in parts of Lancashire and Cumbria did the religious give notable support to the Pilgrimage of Grace. Only in those parts did the people try effectively to reverse the dissolution. In the far north west, it seems, monasticism remained useful and relevant longer than in the rest of England.

Chapter 4
EDUCATION IN THE DIOCESE

"Godliness and good learning" have gone together since the earliest times. The ministry of the Word – in scripture or liturgy – has always called for a literate priesthood. When secular habits of learning were destroyed at the end of the Roman period, the clergy, for nearly a thousand years, provided society with most of the literate men required for the business of government. Even when lay literacy grew in the thirteenth century, the Church and the men of the Church continued to run the schools – and so it remained until little over a hundred years ago.

The evidence for education in Cumbria up to the sixteenth century is tantalisingly thin. We can only guess that some Cumbrians must have gone over the hills to the diocesan school kept by John of Beverley, Bishop of Hexham, in the 680s. We must assume that someone besides the local priest was expected to read the now illegible inscription on the Bewcastle cross, and to pick out the lines of the Dream of the Rood on that at Ruthwell. Some learning must have gone on in the early monasteries at Dacre, Heversham and Carlisle; and with the revival of monasticism in the twelfth century no doubt education in the scriptures, Latin grammar and music would be provided for novices, and perhaps for the children of local gentry and tenants. But the only hard evidence for any monastic school in Cumbria comes from a chance survival in the records, 42 years after the last of the monks left. In 1582, the tenants of the lands of the former Abbey of Furness looked back to the days when the monks had maintained a school to which tenants' sons had been admitted.

We are on firmer ground in tracing a cathedral school at Carlisle. Even if we discount the twelfth century legend that St. Cuthbert founded schools there, a school is reliably mentioned in 1188, and there are other references until 1371, when John of Burdon, "master of the schools of Carlisle", made his will. In 1285, Bishop Ireton tried to endow places for twelve poor scholars in the cathedral school. There is a gap in the record until a grammar school is founded in 1545. There are records of other early schools at Penrith in 1340 and 1395, Cockermouth in the early fourteenth century, Appleby from 1286, Brough in 1506, Kendal in 1527, and possibly at Beetham. A recent study suggests a literacy rate of 10-12% for the north of England by 1500, rising rapidly in the next century.

The First Grammar Schools

Although the monasteries were dissolved by 1540, and the chantries in the next decade, the reformed Church of England remained at the heart of education over the coming centuries. Canon Bouch noted the foundation dates of the network of classical or grammar schools in the Diocese as follows, a majority of them possessing ordained clergymen as masters or ushers (i.e. headmasters and teachers), all heavily weighted on their governing bodies by ecclesiastical influence, and turning out many clergy amongst their scholars; Kirkby Stephen 1566, Keswick 1571, Blencow 1578, Urswick 1580, St. Bees 1583, Hawkshead 1585, Kirkby Lonsdale 1591, Stainmore 1594, Dean 1596, Cartmel pre-1598, Crosby Garrett by 1600, Kirkby Ireleth 1608, Bridekirk 1609, Bromfield 1612, Old Hutton 1613, Heversham 1613, Dalton 1622, Bampton 1627, Addingham 1634, Lowther 1638, Troutbeck 1639, Dendron 1644, Caldbeck 1647, Barton 1650, Ings 1650, Burton 1657, Broughton 1657, Ulverston 1658, Bowness 1665, Kelsick (Ambleside) 1721.

By the late 17th century about 40% of the parishes under the old diocese of Carlisle possessed schoolmasters, whereas in southern Westmorland, under the Diocese of Chester, 70% of parishes seem to have had a resident schoolmaster. All, of course, had to be licensed by the bishop or his appointed deputy, and those considered at all suspect were closed. The growth of population, of wealth, and of lay culture separate from the church encouraged many private schools throughout Cumbrian villages and towns of the late Tudor and Stuart periods, so that there were 19 endowed Grammar, and 25 endowed non-Grammar schools in Cumberland between 1660 and 1800, and 23 and 5 respectively in Westmorland, always better provided for than Cumberland and most other English counties.

The Clergy as Schoolmasters

Clergy frequently acted as village schoolmasters, gaining an extra stipend, pupils' fees or payments in kind to augment a poor income. Clergy also maintained private establishments. There were between 30 and 40 of these in the county directories for the mid-19th century, offering tuition for pupils to go on to major public schools (then much reformed and likewise often church foundations and clerically controlled) or on to Oxford and Cambridge colleges – (especially Queen's Oxford, which still has close Cumbrian links). John Fawcett, the famous incumbent of St. Cuthbert's, Carlisle, and

Walter Fletcher, Vicar of Dalston, coached sons of the gentry and nobility, including titled men including the later Home Secretary and statesman, Sir James Graham of Netherby. There seem to have been about 300 private schools by the mid-19th century in the county, but there were 254 Anglican controlled foundations by 1874 and 338 by 1890.

The Church of England also ran one pioneering institution of university standard in our area: the theological college at St. Bees, which opened in 1816 and closed in 1895. Founded by Bishop Law of Chester, it was the first effective training college for clergy in England, outside the universities of Oxford and Cambridge. In an age when many country parishes were poorly served by ill-paid curates, the incumbents being often absentees, and many town parishes were overwhelmed by the influx of population, it helped to meet a pressing need for more clergy with better education. The college maintained high standards and provided an avenue into the Church for men of all classes.

Education by the Churches

English education suffered difficulties due to religious divisions during the 19th century, and Nonconformists challenged Anglican influence in schools, as elsewhere in intellectual and social life. It is too easy to over-estimate local difficulties, and though these did occur in the diocese, they were nothing like the tremendously bitter antagonisms raised in major urban centres. Schools (called British) for all denominations were established in Appleby, Carlisle, Maryport, and other towns; the Quakers and Methodists had large and educationally important schools at Wigton, Ulverston, Penrith and Barrow; and dissenting ministers and Roman Catholic clergy were deeply committed to education. However, the major burden for educating all people, rich and poor, bright or dull, lay in Cumbria with the Church of England, and in its revived condition of the mid-19th century it responded willingly to the challenge of rapidly growing population, and large new industrial, mining and urban centres, swelled by Irish, Scottish and English migrants in west and south Cumbria.

In the Victorian period, records of Bishop's Visitations provide details on Church schools throughout the region, and illustrate the immense variety of the foundations, their wealth, staff, size, pupils and origins. Lowther and Shap schools were financed by the Earls of Lonsdale for their tenants and labourers, the Howards provided in east Cumberland for their workers and miners, and the Thanet family provided schools in the upper Eden valley. Sir Wilfred

Lawson built schools in Aspatria, and the Victorian landowners generally worked with the Anglican clergy to provide rural schools.
Successive vicars of Holm Cultram gave close oversight to local schools, although there were 14 within the parish, and not all of the teachers responded to clerical comment! Certainly under Bishop Goodwin after 1869 country schools received great impetus, and with the arrival of the first State Board schools, in areas where the various denominations failed to provide sufficient accommodation, the clergy provided intense competition to the State to ensure that Anglican influence was maintained. The real problem for the schools was the continued growth of population, coupled with the agricultural depression of the last quarter of the 19th century which seriously impaired the Church's ability to provide schools for all. Too many people and too little cash forced an understanding between Church and state after the 1890s.

Growth of State Schools

By 1882 elementary education was compulsory to the age of 13, and in 1891 it became free. This, together with rising standards needed for training staff and providing schools of modern design and equipment, created serious financial problems for the diocese. The 1902 Education Act placed Church schools on the local rates, thus relieving them of financial worries but allowing them control of appointments and of religious instruction, ever a bone of contention. Sunday schools naturally had existed under Anglican and Dissenting auspices in Cumbria from the 1780s, with all the main towns possessing large schools within a few years. Yet there was the ever present, very occasionally justified, fear among non-Anglicans of the indoctrination of their children in Anglican ways. The Cowper-Temple clause of 1870 allowed parents to opt out of religious instruction, and further safeguards were applied later. The extensive provision of state elementary schools, especially in towns, and of secondary schools in the 20th century, provided an alternative yet complementary system to that of the Anglican Church, though integration took place in most facets of educational work. The primacy of the Church in its own schools was re-affirmed by the 1944 Education Act, under which schools could be either "controlled" (i.e. financed and controlled by the local authority) or "voluntary aided" (i.e. where the governors provided part of the finance) with some limited independence but within the State system of education. Religious instruction was to be compulsory in Church and State schools, though parents could arrange for their children not to attend this if they so wished.

The Diocesan Education Committee and its school managers supervised the continuing Church schools in the Diocese, and particular attention was given to religious instruction. Strenuous attempts were made to provide as many schools as possible with aided status since this provided greater control for the Church, and much energy has been put into keeping open village schools in order to avoid school amalgamation. By the 1960s about 90 schools were aided and 90 controlled in the Diocese, and continued zeal and activity by the Diocesan authorities eased what could have been difficult relationships with the local education authorities over Church schools. With vigour new schools were opened, or old ones re-built and renovated, between 1950 and 1966 at Selside, Barrow-in-Furness, Scotby, Wiggonby, Calthwaite, Crosthwaite, Skirwith, Ireleth, Orton, Crosby Ravensworth, Stainton, Beckermet, Blackford, Windermere, Natland, Burneside, Mosser, Lazonby, Carlisle, Kendal and Rosley. Alongside these physical manifestations of Church zeal were weekend and longer courses, extensive meetings and consultations and the working of a variety of officials and committees, all devoted to education and the part of the Church of England in it.

The dominant and obvious trend in education at all levels since the 19th century has been the growth of State control in Cumbria, as everywhere else, largely due to fundamental changes and developments in society and the economy, the growth of democracy in government, and individual responsibility within the collective unity of the State. Religious influences had undeniably declined in the face of secular activity, often favouring no religion at all; with the decline in Church revenue, the infinitely superior State resources have increasingly meant that the authority paying also controls what goes on. However, the Church of England remains established and linked with the State; since it has existed, through bad and good times, for some centuries, it seems reasonable to assume that it will continue to exercise a beneficial influence on many pupils of the Diocese, especially when incumbents continue to be so important to the proper functioning of the traditional life of the countryside.

Chapter 5
THE WIDER CHURCH

It is a truism that religion has brought the very best out of men and women, and that it has been responsible for the very worst of human behaviour. Nowhere has this been more the case than in dealings between denominations, though the distressing part has always been that far more unites the major British Christian denominations than ever divided them. In Cumbria arguably the worst of the excesses committed in the name of religion have been absent, though there were both Catholics and Protestants from Cumbria executed for their faith at the time of the Reformation.

After the Reformation a small number of Cumbrian gentry, headed by some of the Howards and Stricklands, and a number of their tenants and servants, continued to worship according to the ways of the Roman church. They were for long regarded as possible or likely traitors, and magistrates like Sir Daniel Fleming of Rydal delighted in hounding suspected "Papists". Until the influx of Irish Roman Catholics in the 1830s and 1840s, native "recusants" or Roman Catholics numbered less than 1% of the population, and possessed less influence and authority than their kin in Lancashire, Durham and Northumberland. The Irish settled in Carlisle, Barrow, Millom and West Cumberland in some numbers, and undoubted instances of religious bigotry and persecution did occur on both sides – Irish attacked a Primitive Methodist congregation in 1851 and a Wesleyan minister in 1816; attacks on the Irish were made on Cleator Moor in the 1880s. There was suspicion between the English and Irish communities, but it was largely because of nationality and accent and habits, not because of religion. There were nearly as many Scottish in Cumbria as Irish-born migrants in 1851, but they did not remain in close-knit communities and were usually better educated and of a higher social and economic status. It must be emphasised that Thomas West, author of the famous guide to Furness, was a highly respected priest in the 1770s, and that his contemporaries at Corby and Dodding Green, before their removal to Carlisle and Kendal respectively, were recognised members of their rural communities.

The Society of Friends

If Roman Catholics did not find Cumbria conducive to their missions, it was exactly the reverse with George Fox in the 1650s

WORKINGTON KESWICK

George Fox
'The Man in
Leather Breeches'

G.E.P.S., 1982

when he allied with the Westmorland Seekers and organised his first 70 Quakers into 35 missionary teams to evangelise Europe, the Americas and Britain. The Quakers of the 17th century were the natural refuge of those who disagreed with the Presbyterian organisation of the Commonwealth under Oliver Cromwell, who nevertheless gave them religious freedom. The Restoration and 30 years of great persecution increased numbers dramatically in Cumberland, Furness and Westmorland.

The magistrates and authorities tried but ultimately failed to root out such unconventional people, who refused to attend church, observe the sacraments, or to acknowledge the authority of the justices, King or clergy. After 1689, apart from occasional disturbances, the Quakers had won their battle to worship as they chose and remained a small but influential sector of society. Schools for all denominations were founded by a Quaker in Whitehaven and Kendal, they were prominent in industry and manufacturing trades, and, by the early 19th century, formed an impressive political force for those seeking freedom from the political control of the Earl of Lonsdale in Kendal and Westmorland. David Butler has lovingly drawn and described their meeting houses such as Swarthmoor, near Ulverston, and Brigflatts near Sedbergh which adorn the county and always seem to fit so perfectly the Cumbrian climate and temperament.

With influence today out of all proportion to their numbers, Quaker thinking underlies modern movements for conservation and nuclear disarmament.

John Wesley and the Methodists

It is also in the nature of denominations that they should co-operate, in spite of their differences. Thus it was that early Methodists of the 18th century were greatly helped in Furness, Dentdale, Gosforth, Hawkshead and many other places by the Quakers, and the new and assertive preachers and evangelists under John Wesley followed in the footsteps of Fox and his determined evangelists a century before. Wesley insisted that he and his few preachers should go not to those who needed them, but to those who needed them most. Wesley was 26 times on Cumbrian soil and was often at Whitehaven. He went through most of our towns and villages, and his tours have been fully recorded. Wesley must have been remarkable not only for his spiritual leadership and preaching, but also for his physical stamina. In 1764, for example, he travelled 1800 miles on horseback between March and August, and preached at 122

John Wesley preaching at Carlisle Cross

towns and villages. His last visit to Kendal was in 1788 when he was 85.

He and his followers created a web of Societies and circuits embracing Cumbria, first based on Whitehaven, in the 1800s Carlisle, and the Methodists established chapels and attracted hearers and members in numbers second only to the Church of England. Disagreements amongst the Wesleyans of the 19th century created Primitive Methodists, Bible Christians, Methodist New Connexion, and United Methodist Free Church Connexions (of churches), all organised differently, yet all able to re-unite in 1932 because their basic doctrine and beliefs were so similar.

The Methodists posed as serious contenders in the early 19th century for the title of new "established Church", and, because of their success, the Church of England was forced to reform its anachronistic features over the next half century to combat the challenge. Religion and the nation benefited from these. In Cumbria the Methodists built over 300 places of worship, which remain today for us to admire; they brought evangelical religion, higher educational aspirations and self-esteem to common people; they forced other denominations to be on their mettle and to infuse new enjoyment into religious occasions; they exemplified a new attitude to morality. The Methodists were active in providing Sunday Schools, and encouraged the acquisition of business and organisational skills among chapel members. Above all, the Methodists encouraged the involvement of two groups in worship who had been previously neglected; women, and the laity. Laymen preached in churches, and women were encouraged (most of all in Primitive ranks) to do all that men were doing. It was no coincidence that the reforming Bishops – Villiers, Waldegrave and Goodwin – should wish to emulate their success by taking the laity into the running of the diocesan machinery and into the full life of their Church. It was in a way unfortunate that for so long the Church of England was regarded as a body imposed from above on those below, financed, organised and controlled by the upper echelons of society, whereas the Nonconformists provided their religion and their buildings from below. Whilst the Dukes of Devonshire and Buccleuch provided Anglican churches for Barrow-in-Furness, miners and poor farmers in Alston were gathering cobbles from the burns for their chapel's walls, and quarry workers at Shap went begging from door to door to buy materials for the Methodist chapel foundations.

The Other Free Churches

The Nonconformist Churches provided lively worship, charity for the poor and the means of social advancement. There were many

Baptist congregations in the Diocese, notably those at Gt. Broughton, Maryport, Barrow-in-Furness, Hawkshead Hill, Torver, Whitehaven, Kirkby Stephen and in a number of villages and towns, some permanently established, others merely temporary. There were not as many congregations of Baptists as there were of Congregationalists (about 60 places of worship in the 1870s) or Presbyterians (around 35 places of worship) in Cumbria. In 1972 the Presbyterian Church of England and the Congregational Church in England and Wales amalgamated to form the United Reformed Church. Some local Congregational churches chose to remain outside the Union, but all the Presbyterian congregations became part of the wider Church. The Presbyterians were largely influenced by the proximity to the Border, and a supply of Scottish ministers looked after the English and Scottish communities – the Scottish ones for instance in Barrow, Longtown, Brampton and Kendal, the English ones at Gt. Salkeld, Silloth and Distington. The Baptists tended to be poorer congregations, the poor relations in a way of the Congregational and Presbyterian hearers who were typically tradesmen, shopkeepers and merchants like the Carr family of Carlisle. Yet all had their own chapels and forms of worship and beliefs that bore great similarities to each other, and it was this recognition of basic similarity which allowed exchanges of pulpits, ministers" "fraternals" and similar co-operative ventures in the later 19th century, and a generally excellent relationship with the Methodists.

This by no means exhausts the non-Anglican denominations of the religiously pluralistic 19th century society; Bible Christians, mainly Cornishmen, in Barrow, Dalton, Askam, Swarthmoor, Haverigg, Millom, Cleator Moor, Ravenglass, Moor Row; Unitarians in Kendal, Carlisle and Cleator; Welsh Calvinistic Methodists in Barrow, Dalton and Millom; Inghamite, Church of Christ and a variety of Brethren in the towns; the Salvation Army, after 1880, evangelising major centres, and a variety of missions into the 20th century touring or operating from urban bases, throughout the Diocese. Each had a distinctive attitude towards its role and work, yet their similarities were greater than their differences. It was unfortunate that these bonds of brotherhood were long obscured by differences in politics, which left the tradition of Nonconformity being synonymous with Liberalism, Anglicanism with the Conservatives, and allowed issues like education to prevent closer communion.

Chapter 6
THE INDUSTRIAL REVOLUTION AND THE 19th CENTURY IN CUMBRIA

The modern age has its roots in the 18th and 19th centuries, times of great social and economic development, whose impact and implications are even now not fully understood or appreciated. Out of the stresses and strains of large scale demographic changes, mining, industrial and agricultural innovations, and the rise of large urban centres, was created the new society in which we find ourselves, and we are the inheritors of the world created by those most impatient, energetic and eager beings, the Victorians.

Agriculture and the Enclosures

When Bailly and Cully toured Cumbria for the Board of Agriculture in the 1790s, they reported that the region was generally backward but improving. The so-called "Revolution", which had been in progress and was gathering momentum for several decades, accelerated into the new century. Huge areas of common grazing were enclosed. Although the effects of this enclosure movement between 1770 and 1830 have been fiercely disputed, there is no denying that they made agriculture more efficient. Once enclosed in fields, huge tracts of land were either brought under arable cultivation or put under grass after draining and improving, and devoted to cattle and sheep. There were a number of major improving landlords – the Howards of Greystoke, Corby and Naworth, the Grahams of Netherby, Henry Curwen and his son-in-law and nephew John Christian Curwen near Workington, and the Lowther family in Westmorland and West Cumberland.

They used competent and trained land agents to encourage, cajole or threaten tenants to adopt modern methods, against the weight of tradition and inertia. The landless labourers were to provide a huge population surplus to feed the growing towns, and, throughout the 19th century, there was a continuous stream of migrants to the colonies in search of better things. By the 1880s even the pastoral economy of much of Cumbria was feeling the ill-effects of the great depression in agriculture which so reduced Church income, and times for farmers and landlords were precarious into the 1920s.

New Industries

The countryside since enclosure has drastically altered, but it was the industrial development and urban expansion which so amazed contemporaries who witnessed the changes. The factory system first affected the textile trades, and by the last quarter of the 18th century Wigton, Dalston and the Calder valley, Carlisle and Longtown had experienced textile expansion and the coming of the factory system, which eventually replaced the old domestic system by the mid-19th century. At the same time peace on the Border, for the first time in centuries, encouraged the rapid expansion of Carlisle city boundaries. The role of the city as an administrative and communications centre received fresh impetus from the first railways of the 1830s, and even from the ill-fated Carlisle canal to Port Carlisle on the Solway. Whitehaven had been the economic boom town of the 18th century, with its vast coal measures and major port status, but it was replaced by the better sited Carlisle, which attracted up-and-coming entrepreneurs in biscuits, cottons, hats, iron and steel construction, engineering, and even whip making.

The coal and iron ore mines of West Cumberland provided livelihoods for thousands of people, in scores of mining settlements which sprang up where previously merely a hamlet existed – Rowrah, Egremont, Arlecdon, Moor Row, Kirkland, Cleator, Brigham, Camerton, Bigrigg, Beckermet, Moresby, Distington, Clifton, Broughton, Dearham, and others. They were often ancient settlements, even with castle and parish church, but their mining interests multiplied the population, sometimes twenty-fold in ten years. Whitehaven remained a major centre, whilst Workington rose to prominence with Cammell's iron company removing from Dronfield, in search of lower overheads and transport costs, in the 1870s.

Further down the coast, Millom, formerly a pleasant rural community under the eye of the old castle, blossomed forth in the 1860s, when the nation's largest deposit of haematite was discovered and mined during the 1860s, and 10,000 migrants made it prosper. Not far away, Barrow-in-Furness, described as the "Wild West Town" of Britain, became a major iron, steel, shipbuilding and engineering centre from the 1850s onwards, and provided Cumbria with its second largest urban centre. Westmorland's industrial development was much more modest, though Kendal remained a prosperous community, replacing Appleby in all but name and official functions as county centre. A group of later Victorian seaside and retirement resorts – Grange-over-Sands, Arnside, Silloth, Seascale, St. Bees, complete the major changes of the 19th century.

The Beginning of Tourism

Cumbria was one of the first regions to experience a phenomenon common to most beautiful areas; an invasion of tourists, presenting

a dire threat to its natural resources and giving rise to issues, campaigns and bodies which will be dealt with in another chapter. Suffice it to say that there were plenty of wealthy tourists disturbing the Lake Poets and their circle before 1820. Radically improved communications – railways to Windermere in the 1840s, to Keswick in the 1860s, and earlier along the western coast, as well as good turnpike roads built during the late 18th century – brought in large numbers of day trippers, who swamped certain centres, and allowed the affluent to commute to their sources of wealth in the industrial centres, whilst keeping an establishment in the Lake District. Naturally, many valleys and mountains remained peaceful until the age of the internal combustion engine rudely awakened them to modern realities, but the Lakes had well and truly succumbed to their "discovery" by the Victorians. Most obviously the "invaders" built on a lavish scale; gargantuan hotels in Keswick, Bowness, Windermere, Grasmere and even down Borrowdale, nowhere was safe. Hundreds of terraced guest houses catered for the less socially exclusive; and the inevitable rows of "villas", not discreetly situated, but boldly asserting their prominence, were built facing a favoured view, and mainly around Windermere itself. Town facilities were expanded, shops and traders did well, roads were laid, paved and drained, and many like Harriett Martineau, the Unitarian journalist at "The Knoll", Ambleside, were delighted that so much of "civilised living" had permeated even the Lakes. Above all the Victorians built, altered or restored their churches with a passion bordering on mania, and in so devastating a manner that much historical evidence was destroyed in the process.

New Challenges to the Churches

The challenge of all these changes to the Church of England can be imagined. The Church possessed an inflexible parochial structure, which made creating and financing new parishes and churches awkward and contentious, but where the people now were, the clergy often were not. Nonconformity had few of these problems, and benefited greatly from Anglican ineptitude but, by the 1860s, reforming bishops and zealous clergy and laymen and women redressed the balance and went to extraordinary lengths to provide church accommodation, in the belief that lack of provision deterred hearers from attending worship. Between 1747 and 1840 there were 21 new churches built in Cumbria and major repair or restoration work at 50 others; in the period 1840 to 1856 27 new churches were built and 16 restored, whilst under Bishops Villiers and Waldegrave 47 new ones were built and 65 restored (1857/69). These two men

were aristocratic evangelicals, who carried out initial modernization work in the Diocese, after the passing of the "High and Dry" Bishop Percy, who had delayed the merging of the Chester Deaneries with Carlisle for 20 years.

Their vigour was followed by an equally reforming and modernising prelate, Harvey Goodwin, described as moderately High Church (as was his son-in-law, Henry Ware, Bishop Suffragan of Barrow-in-Furness). From 1869 to 1892 64 new churches were built and 96 others received major restoration work at an estimated cost of about £350,000, a colossal sum in Victorian terms. At the same time, attention was given to Church schools, parsonages and halls, many of which continue in use today. Goodwin in particular was keen to attract qualified clergy – graduates of the universities or theological colleges rather than simply literates – and to make sure that the cathedral played an active part as the mother church of the region.

Cumbria's churches are a fine heritage, and an endless source of delight to visit. National figures worked on our churches: Robert Smirke on Crosby Ravensworth, and Askham, as well as Edmond Castle and public buildings in Carlisle; Thomas Rickman on Holy Trinity, Carlisle (recently demolished), and on work for Bishop Percy at Rose Castle; John Dobson of Newcastle fame, at Warwick; Butterfield, the High Church restorer and much in favour with the Earls of Lonsdale, at St. Bees; as well as a number of county men such as Hodgson of Carlisle and Webster of Kendal.

However, church building was so important in the Victorian age that further words need to be written about two important firms and one individual, who brought something special to the Diocese. The individual was Philip Webb, who in the 1870s was a famous architect working for many patrons, amongst the most devoted being the Howards, Earls of Carlisle. By that date the heir was breaking with tradition and living with his own family at Naworth Castle. Webb was responsible for a most interesting and original church at Brampton, and for having superb stained glass by Morris and Burne Jones. It was Webb's only church, and illustrates the close connection between the Howards of that time and the pre-Raphaelite movement. Further stained glass by Morris and Burne Jones was placed in Kirkbampton, Staveley, Troutbeck, Ponsonby and Lanercost (due to the Howards being patrons of the living). However, Henry Holiday copied Burne Jones and produced in a dozen churches excellent quality glass including Wythburn, Muncaster, and Ponsonby, with many other firms active but not producing such high quality material.

The two firms who deserve special mention are C. J. Ferguson, of Carlisle, and Paley and Austin of Lancaster. Charles Ferguson went into partnership with John Cory in the 1860s, Cory ultimately concentrating on his practice in the North East (whilst Cumberland county surveyor), and Ferguson, brother of the historian and Chancellor R. S. Ferguson, doing most work in Cumbria. Ferguson was architect for Silloth, Pooley Bridge, Bridekirk, Cumdivock, Gamblesby, St. Aidan (Carlisle), Penruddock, Burneside, Middleton, Sebergham, Plumbland, and Welton, and, as Diocesan Surveyor until his death in 1904, advised on work being carried out in scores of county churches. Nikolaus Pevsner thought highly of him, regarding him as one of the best regional architects, with a sympathetic manner in restoring old or neglected fabrics.

Edmund Sharpe of Lancaster took into partnership E. G. Paley in 1845, in order to allow himself time for his absorbing hobbies. Paley, grandson of the eminent Archdeacon Paley of Carlisle, had a free hand in matters after Sharpe's virtual retirement in 1851, but when Paley took H. J. Austin into partnership in 1868, the latter transformed the firm into a major regional business, responsible for hundreds of churches, mansions and public buildings in the north of England into the 20th century. Paley died in 1895, and the firm became Austin and Paley, with Paley junior working with Austin. Pevsner described their work as amongst the very best in England, full of resourcefulness, invention and nobility, which today can be seen at St. James (Barrow), Flookburgh, St. Mary, (Dalton-in-Furness), Broughton East, Finsthwaite, Torver, and throughout South Cumbria and Lancashire. They also built part of Leighton Hall and re-built Holker for the Dukes of Devonshire, after a disastrous fire.

The Victorians were responding to new pressures and problems, and to an extent solved or avoided them, occasionally failing to gauge what was required of their Church. Their heritage nonetheless is a rich and noble one, and there is a compelling atmosphere when entering any of their church buildings, even in such tiny edifices as Eskdale, Wythburn or Newlands. They left problems for us – huge, expensive vicarages and a network of churches depending on liberal use of manpower. They built into their churches what they believed needed emphasising in religion, forgetting that future generations would invariably wish to adapt and alter; but they left a glorious heritage for us to enjoy in this modern Diocese.

Chapter 7
THE LAKE DISTRICT AND THE DIOCESE

The Lake District was not always regarded as a marvellous region; John Wesley and earlier travellers regarded it as an area fraught with bad weather, awkward and "primitive" inhabitants, and appalling roads, doubly cursed with marshy water-filled valleys and huge forbidding mountains. This view gradually changed into the cult of the "picturesque" and the "romantic" helped by the influence of the poet Gray and the Lake Poets and their friends and admirers.

The Coming of the Railways

Before the 1840s there had been two generations of settlers domiciled alongside, but not integrated with, the native populace. They included the nobility, deprived of the European Grand Tour by the unsettled state of Europe between 1793 and 1815 and periodically thereafter; curious foreigners; and the newly affluent business, professional and intellectual classes who sought, like the Arnolds of Fox Howe and Harriet Martineau of the Knoll, a peaceful home away from the increasingly large, unfriendly and ugly, urban spheres of their activity. It provided a welcome retreat from the world in the most remote corner of England, which had the added bonus of a coterie of poets. As the century wore on railways reached into, and created, the town of Windermere in 1847, came to Coniston in 1859, to Keswick by 1863, with lines to Lakeside, and Eskdale.

Thousands of cheap day returns brought the poorer people of industrial Lancashire, Yorkshire and Tyneside to the locality, and further railway schemes to dissect Lakeland caused the creation of the Lake District Defence League to prevent incursions during the 1880s. Ultimately the National Trust developed from these efforts to preserve some beauty and remoteness for people to enjoy in an unspoilt area of Britain, and Canon Hardwick Drummond Rawnsley, Vicar of Crosthwaite, was the lynchpin for the activities of all the defenders in the period 1880 to 1920.

Lakeland became a playground for the nation, though less commercialised than the seaside resorts, and thus gave rise to the first major and successful preservation and conservation groups. It also continued to be an area of agriculture, of industry and mining, industries which managed to survive both preservationist and exploitationist encounters. The problem of maintaining a balance without making the region a huge museum rather than a living and working entity remains; what concerns this chapter is the association of religion with the Lakes.

Wordsworth

The association of religious experience with the wild mountains and lakes of Cumbria really starts with William Wordsworth, the one native Lake poet. He was much more akin in his attitudes and prejudices to his fellow Cumbrians than he ever was to Southey, Coleridge and company, in his dislike of tourists and visitors and his desire to keep the Lakes free of interference by economic exploiters. Yet it is Wordsworth who continues to attract hosts of curious or venerating tourists year after year, as he was doing in the 1800s. It was he who held forth on the revelation of religious experience through the beauty of the Lakes, creating a "religion of nature" as Norman Nicholson writes, covering the fells and dales in the "comfortable warmth of religiosity". It was easy for the Lakers to confuse the exhilaration of climbing with the fervour of religious experience, and to read in wild nature evangelical messages of religious devotion. The early Victorians came to worship Wordsworth and his poetry, and to seek in the Lakes a rest cure from the anxieties of an urbanising and industrial age, a purification and cleansing process, half physical, half religious in tone.

Ruskin

It was William Ruskin who made the Lakes conform to views suggested by interpreters of Wordsworth's words, and who became the sage of the late Victorian and 20th century generations. He retired to Brantwood on Coniston to seek respite from a highly successful public life and completely disastrous private one; he found consolation and fulfilment in the Lakes, and encouraged many others to do so. The goal of many then, and now, was, and is, to own a house and to live in the Lakes. Ruskin was held responsible for reintroducing the element of the mysterious and supernatural into an increasingly materialistic religion of the day, and for making religion into something which could only be understood by experiencing the thrill of the Lake District and its "revealed religion". Ruskin, like Wordsworth, was a great moral teacher, and his classroom was the Lakes.

The Keswick Convention

The Lakes have meant a good deal to the actively religious of this nation, not only because of Wordsworth and Ruskin, but because of T. D. Harford Battersby, Vicar of St. John's, Keswick, and founder, with Robert Wilson, a Brigham Quaker, of the Keswick Convention.

Battersby had flirted with the Tractarian movement in the 1840s at Oxford, before coming as curate to Frederick Myers, the Vicar of Keswick, in 1849. Both men found evangelical religion increasingly attractive, but Myers died young and Battersby replaced him as Vicar in 1851, becoming a well-known and influential evangelical in a Diocese long known for its very Low Church tendencies. Increasingly attracted to the idea of conventions, or meetings, for the pursuit of "holiness", both personally and as part of a group, Battersby was able, in spite of many opponents, to inaugurate the Keswick Convention in 1875, and it has been held ever since during July. By his death in 1883 the Convention had become established, with representatives from all over Britain mixing with increasing numbers of foreign Christians of all denominations. The Convention maintained close links between Britain and the U.S.A., with the Commonwealth, and with organisations of a similar religious tone, such as the Y.M.C.A., with which both Villiers and Waldegrave had been closely connected. As part of Keswick fortnight the attenders would not only take part in worship and meetings in town and tent, but would actively explore the surrounding countryside, revelling in the capricious July weather, regarding it as intimately bound up with the "Keswick experience". The crusty Archbishop Thomson of York, a native of Whitehaven and in permanent conflict with his Dean and other High Church clergy, enjoyed regular walking and rowing on Derwentwater during the late 1870s and early 1880s.

It is unfortunate and confusing that over the past two centuries so many have been willingly and happily tricked into regarding the Lakes as a place to worship, and the scenery and hills almost as so many idols to revere. It remains a matter of personal judgement and opinion how far the Lakes should be regarded as the ideal place for Christian worship, though their impact on religion is undeniably strong.

Chapter 8
THE MINISTRY OF THE PARISH CLERGY

All through the centuries the worship and ministry of the clergy has continued, providing in each town and village dedicated men, often greatly helped by their wives, serving their God and their parish. Always at hand in times of sickness or bereavement, they have set an example of dedication and service in an increasingly materialistic world.

Their names are recorded in many churches on painted boards, sometimes going back hundreds of years, but their service and value is seldom recorded. A few examples may give some flavour of their contribution to Cumbrian life.

"Wonderful Walker"

Robert Walker, 1709-1802, was born in Seathwaite, the youngest of 12 children, and received his education from the curate of Loweswater. At the age of 26 he became Curate of Seathwaite, and for the rest of his life served his community as parson, schoolmaster, doctor and wise counsellor. He ran his own farm and sheared his own sheep on a stone slab, still to be seen outside his church.

> "His seat was within the rails of the altar, the communion table was his desk . . . and he employed himself at the spinning wheel, while the children were repeating their lessons by his side."

His stipend initially was £5 a year and his cottage, rising after 19 years to £20. He made no charge for his schoolmastering but "such as could afford gave him what they pleased". He was expert on plants, fossils and astronomy. His wife died at the age of 93, and he died a few months later at the same age.

Wordsworth describes his saintly, simple life in "The Excursion" and the Duddon Sonnets.

The Church and Football

Norman Nicholson's splendid anthology, "The Lake District", contains a lively portrait of the 18th century Rector of Ousby, near Penrith, the Reverend Thomas Robinson, who was "beloved, respected, and also a man of humour".

"It was his constant practice, after Sunday afternoon prayers, to accompany the leading men of his parish to the adjoining ale-house, when each man spent a penny, and only a penny; that done he set the younger men to play at football (of which he was a great promoter) and other rustical diversions."

John Baycliffe, born at Appleby in 1868, was brought up in the deeply held Primitive Methodist tradition, the son and grandson of local preachers. He began preaching at 17, and dedicated himself to full-time evangelism – in the North East, in Bristol and in Manchester. When he died in 1950 he left behind memories of a devoted evangelist and man of prayer.

In St. John's Church, Hutton Roof, is recorded a former Vicar, the Reverend T. B. Hardy, who, as a Chaplain in the 1914-18 war, was awarded the Victoria Cross, as well as the D.S.O. and M.C., fearlessly going out night after night to bring in wounded men. He was killed shortly before the war ended.

Market St. Chapel in Kendal was the scene of two remarkable dissenting ministries in the eighteenth century. It was a time of acute and sometimes bitter theological controversy, but the selfless service, Christlike character and scholarly quality of the two Caleb Rotherhams, father and son, from 1716 to 1796 made a profound and lasting impression on the church life of Westmorland.

At the end of the First World War the saintly A. B. Marshall, Congregational minister of Anthorn, after thirty-seven years as pastor in that one place, was still tramping nine miles each Sunday at the age of eighty to conduct services and superintend Sunday Schools in three places, for a stipend of £40 a year and the use of a tied manse.

The Reverend James Birkett Clark was another greatly-loved minister in Cumberland. After serving as a missionary in Papua New Guinea for twenty-five years he came to Keswick in 1931, and soon endeared himself as unofficial Father-in-God to the scattered small church of the Cumberland District of the old Lancashire Congregational Union. A wise and gentle counsellor and friend to ministers and fellowships alike, he was an example of the gifted but unassuming minister, who in every denomination, enriches and strengthens not only his own flock but the whole community in which his life is set.

Every church and chapel must have its own records and memories of its clergy, present as well as past, and of the rich variety of their lives of devotion and service. They still maintain the continuity of worship, of spiritual leadership and of practical service. It is, sadly, often only when parishes have to be amalgamated or churches closed that people realise just how much their own vicar or priest or minister meant to them.

The Continuity of Worship

The Bible links all the Christian Churches, and has had a profound effect on our lives, our speech, our laws and our literature. At the centre of every Christian community the regular daily and weekly services continue, when the Bible is read and expounded, and where Christians meet to worship God, to pray, to learn, to gain fresh strength and encouragement, and to renew their fellowship.

It is rewarding to visit an old parish church and to find in the vestry great old Bibles, the pages worn and torn after years of service on the lectern, and to think of all the past generations of clergy, church-wardens and readers who have turned those pages as they read the lessons. You may find, too, old service books, with the names of past benefactors written in them and old hymn books, now discarded as later generations have sought to find new words and music with which to praise God.

Music has made a great contribution to Christian worship, from the unaccompanied plain-song of the monks, through the long, unbroken tradition of chanting the psalms, to the confident hymns of the Victorians and the syncopated, rhythmic compositions of our own time. The assorted instruments of local musicians, not always in tune, were replaced by the organ, sometimes by the harmonium. It is good to see instruments coming back into use in services, even if they are not always in tune!

Cumbria has a strong musical tradition of choirs and choral societies, of music festivals and concerts, and fine music can be heard all through the year, not just in the Cathedral and in the large town churches, but also in some of the smallest parish churches, as part of their ministry to those on holiday.

The celebration of the Holy Eucharist or Mass is for many Christians the supreme unifying sacrament, where we come together to take the Bread and Wine in memory of Christ's sacrifice. Christians in Cumbria look for the day when all Christians can unite round the altar to celebrate together. Already in Cumbria Churches exchange pulpits, share services, work together and organise joint activities, but there is still much more to be done.

Great efforts have been made to make Church services more appealing to the young and to the uncommitted, to give a warmer welcome to visitors, and to dispel the idea that there is nothing joyful about religion. New translations of the Bible, new forms of service, and new ways of preaching the Gospel through radio and television, are stirring fresh thought and activity. Gerald Priestland's radio series and book "Priestland's Progress" generated new interest in religion among many who have not been to Church in years, while giving new insight and impetus to churchgoers who may have got into a routine.

The Churches in Cumbria have a special duty to serve the thousands of tourists who visit the Lake District every year, to make them welcome, and to demonstrate how full of life and value services can be, whether in the Cathedral, ancient Priory, Roman Catholic or Anglican parish church, Methodist, Baptist, or United Reformed Chapel, Friends Meeting House, or out of doors during some special event such as a Deanery or Diocesan Festival. The collaboration of the Cumbria Tourist Board with the Diocese in 1983 in producing a Christian Heritage map, as part of the 850th Anniversary celebrations, may encourage both visitors and Cumbrian residents to respond to the sound of the church bells.

Chapter 9
THE MODERN AGE

According to John Gay's book, "A Geography of Religion", Cumbria remains one of the most overtly religious regions of England in terms of attendance at worship. A county which is still largely rural retains conservative habits and old traditions, often for the good, whilst large urban centres are more "progressive" and radical in their attitudes and actions. Yet a majority, the overwhelming majority, do not attend any place of worship regularly, and once reliable sources of religious influence, like Sunday Schools, are often a shadow of their original selves. This century has seen two major wars, which robbed Britain of two generations of young people, and accumulated debts of incalculable harm to future generations. The present county has to come to terms with nuclear power, of almost limitless potential for harm and good, on our own doorstep; grave economic and social problems stemming from unemployment, conflict between need for economic development on the one side and conservation and preservation on the other; and difficulties over moral issues which question the relevance and need for Christian-based education, yet which are insoluble by secular means as our governments and councils have discovered.

Naturally, every age has had its problems, and doubtless in a further 850 years' time there will be ones as remote from our difficulties, as ours are from those of the Normans and Anglo-Saxons in 1133 A.D. Perhaps people remain covertly religious, still wishing to take advantage of the Christian rites at birth, marriage and death as an insurance policy into the beyond. Religious instruction is the only compulsory school subject, yet it is one with a chronic shortage of trained specialist staff, and the corporate act of worship often degenerates into a useful opportunity to discipline children. Our whole legal system is based on Christianity, as is our mode of life and culture, but never have our institutions experienced such stresses and strains in modern times. Family life and general moral standards have decayed to a point where Victorians, even Georgians, would have believed themselves on a different planet had they come back to life, whilst Cumbria continues to reflect national trends in crime and social problems such as drink, drugs and gambling.

This is a biassed picture and one way of looking at things. The historian's task is to keep things in perspective. It is a salutary reminder to us in our depressed times to realise that past ages have endured incredible problems, which make one wonder how Christian civilisation has survived. Imagine the gloomy outlook for a fifth-century Christian in Carlisle, seeing society break up under the pressure of warring kingdoms and pirate raids; yet Christianity survived in the Solway basin. Imagine the courage it must have taken a Christian in the tenth century to hold to his faith among Scandinavian incomers whose heroes were Odin and Sigurd; yet the incomers were won over. Imagine the challenge to the Normans of the twelfth century to transform the mud and thatch churches, and to establish still stricter standards of monasticism in the empty coastlands and mountain valleys. Imagine the disappointment of one who had known the peace of the late thirteenth century, like Stephen of Gilling, only to see the start of the age of Border warfare and the construction of fortress churches like Newton Arlosh. Imagine the heartbreak of those who in a conservative area still found the cult of saints and the ministry of monasteries relevant, and saw the King's officers sweep them away; yet on the whole the church adapted peacefully to the new order. Problems are relative, and we need to keep ours in perspective.

It is indeed ironic that, in the most prosperous of conditions ever known to Cumbrians, Christianity should appear to be so neglected. Yet it possesses an inner strength and resilience which continues to make it a formidable influence in our lives. It is beyond reasonable doubt that Christianity in Cumbria, though it will have to alter in many ways in its response and attitudes, will continue to be a vital and healthy force in the future centuries as it has been over the past sixteen.

THE PRESENT AND FUTURE OF THE CARLISLE DIOCESE

by Canon David Jenkins, Secretary of the Diocesan Synod

There are many who believe that the story of the last twenty-five years has been one of retreat – falling numbers, declining incomes, churches declared redundant, vicarages sold, fewer men ordained – a story of general decline. There has been profound questioning of basic Christian doctrines, and, indeed, of man's whole religious experience. The publication of books like "Honest to God" and "God's Dead" did affect the confidence of some Church people. But has this been the story of the Diocese of Carlisle during this period?

Bricks, Mortar and Money

Let's begin with bricks and mortar. During this period we have built 4 new churches, 50 new schools and 38 vicarages, and there have been substantial improvements to church buildings during this period at Haverthwaite; Netherton; St. John's Windermere; St. John the Baptist, Carlisle; St. Thomas Kendal; Dalton-in-Furness; and St. Cuthbert's Carlisle (Tithe Barn). In addition, all over the Diocese, parish churches have been lovingly cared for and restored – not exactly the picture of a church that is fighting a last desperate battle for survival. In fact, the Church of England Year Book for 1981 shows that, as far as Baptisms and Confirmations are concerned, Carlisle Diocese came near the top of the league.

Again the incomes of parishes, far from declining, have steadily increased. In 1961 the Diocesan budget was £58,759, in 1982 it was £1,420,142. While not wanting to suggest that the parishes have had to face no difficulties, the story is not one of unrelieved gloom, nor is it one of general decline.

Pastoral and Administrative Reform

What then had been the strength of the Diocese during the difficult 'sixties and the stormy 'seventies? In our judgement, where it has always been during the long story of the Church in Cumbria, in the parishes. Parish people are the strength of the Diocese, with their faith, their love and their commitment to our Lord and his Church. Because of the strength in the parishes we have been helped by administrative reform, enabling the Diocese to make better use of its resources in manpower, money, land and buildings.

The Pastoral Measure has meant that the Diocese has been able to maintain a pastoral ministry in the rural heartlands of Cumbria, and in key centres to develop team ministries. Groups of clergy, in some cases based on a country town, serve the district around, as at Kirkby Lonsdale, and in towns like Whitehaven and Cockermouth. At Greystoke, following the closure of the pre-theological training school, a team ministry has been established, in which the Chaplain for Agriculture and Rural Life is based. It is hoped that this will become a centre for training in Rural Ministry – an interesting and exciting development.

Synodical Government

The Synodical Government Measure has established a system of Church Government in which the key role of the laity has been recognised. This system is sometimes criticised, but without it we do not believe the Church would have been as successful in raising the substantial sums of money needed to maintain the parochial ministry. In the early 1960s the Church Commissioners provided 80 to 90% of the cost of the ministry, but now the parishes are finding 60%, or over £600,000 in 1982. The Diocese could not have made demands of this scale without parish people having an effective voice in Church government. We believe people of Cumbria have responded to this challenge because they were given a choice. For instance, in 1982, if you want to keep your parson it will cost you £3,700. Many village communities have gladly responded to this challenge. In the past they had lost their village bobby, their village school and their village pub – with very little consultation – but the Church has given them a choice and the response has been very encouraging.

Conference Centres

Three other comparatively recent developments have been of immense value in the Diocese – the Youth Centre at St. John's-in-the-Vale opened in 1951; the Conference Centre at Rydal Hall opened in 1963, and subsequently its campsite and Youth Centre; and most recently, the Coniston Youth Centre. Generations of young people have had the joy of living, working and worshipping at St. John's-in-the-Vale. Rydal Hall has become a great asset for the Diocese and its parishes, as well as for universities, schools and the community at large. The Reverend David Dixon's ministry at Rydal has been of great significance, through his own hard work he has made it a successful enterprise in every way. We now own Rydal because of the foresight of Bishop Cyril Bulley. A measure of that success is the number of individuals, who having first visited Rydal as part of a group, now return year after year during the holiday season. Coniston has only just begun its story, but already it is beginning to make an effective contribution to the young people in Cumbria.

Partners in Mission

After 850 years the Church is very much alive in Cumbria, but of course, bricks and mortar are not the heart of the matter, that must be our Lord and His mission to the whole world, in which we are privileged to share. In 1979 we invited three Dioceses to take part in a Partners in Mission Consultation – Madras, in the Church of South India; Stavanger, part of the Lutheran Church in Norway, with whom our young people already had many links; and Zululand, an Anglican Diocese in South Africa, with whom we were linked in the Mothers Union Wave of Prayer. Before the Partners came we encouraged parishes and deaneries to look at themselves and their strategy for mission.

The Partners arrived in May 1979, and very soon we knew that the Holy Spirit was moving with them in towns, villages and across the fells of Cumbria, changing atitudes. The exercise reached a climax in the Consultation held in Carlisle, based on the Cathedral, St. Cuthbert's Church and the Tithe Barn. The Bishop of Madras called it "a mountain top experience", another Pentecost. But he soon reminded us that we must go back down from the mountain to the valley bottom, and try and be faithful to a vision of the people of God renewed for mission. In the Consultation three key areas in mission were identified – Evangelism, Service to the Community and the World, and the struggle for a Just Society. In their Report our Partners left behind them their wishes for the Diocese of Carlisle.

To share an experience of this sort can be the most wonderful thing for those taking part in it, but have there been any lasting effects? Yes, we believe there have been. Parishes have looked again at their priorities and, as a result, in many places there has been a re-shaping of parish strategy, emphasising mission and outreach. One development has been the Lent Study Course. The first two in 1979 and 1980 were linked to the Partners in Mission Consultation – the first, preparation for the exercise, and the second an attempt to come to terms with the Partners' report. Each year since 1979 there have been Study Courses, and there are many parishes who now have small groups meeting regularly, never having had a study group before. This is a small but significant step forward. In the

northern half of the Diocese local radio, BBC Radio Cumbria, has featured the Lent Course and linked parishes together.

Clergy and Lay Training

The need for training of clergy and laity was also emphasised in the report. The clergy in 1980 had gathered for a successful Clergy School at Ripon – no new thing this for them. As a result of the expectations awakened by the Partners in Mission Consultation and the success of the Clergy School at Ripon, there came a demand from the laity for their own lay training school. And so, in the Spring of 1982, 150 lay people went to Ripon. From it has come a clear call for shared ministry, so that the whole body of Christ can accept responsibility for carrying on the mission of God, and that where possible this should be ecumenical. They asked for continuing help with the study of the Bible so that it might become an inspiration for their life in the world. They expressed the hope that more lay people might take part in the planning of worship. They discovered at Ripon that through a great act of worship the imagination and the understanding of the individual may be quickened. There was a recognition, too, that any action by Church people must be supported and sustained by prayer. This conference could well determine the pattern of ministry that will take the Church in Cumbria into the 21st century.

One of the wishes of our Partners was for closer links with other Christian churches in Cumbria. Informal and friendly links already exist, but there are few major areas of co-operation. The failure of the General Synod in July, 1982 to give the necessary majority in favour of the Covenanting proposals appeared a major set-back to hopes of greater unity, but there is a determination in most parishes in the Diocese to show in practical ways their desire for closer co-operation with other Churches, for joint prayer and worship, and for greater understanding.

On many fronts the Church in Cumbria is alive and continuing to work for the establishment of Christ's Kingdom in our villages and towns. One of the most reassuring signs is the number of Christians who hold responsible positions in the community, giving dedicated service in all walks of life – schools, hospitals, factories, offices, old people's clubs, youth clubs. What begins at the altar table each Sunday is fulfilled in the places where they live and work. One can be certain that the story of Christ in Cumbria is far from finished, indeed the Church is, we believe, better equipped to fulfil its mission now than it has been for many years. So we can look forward to the twenty-first century with confidence.

POSTSCRIPT

by The Right Reverend George Hacker, Bishop of Penrith

To write a Postscript properly you need to read what is written first! I have done this, and I must say it has been an easy and exciting thing to do. So if you are cheating and are starting this book at the wrong end (as people sometimes do, especially with "thrillers"), please go back to the beginning. You will not of course have been expecting a "thriller" when you bought this book, but you won't find it a dull old history book either, or a book just about old churches. I find it is a "thriller" in its own way – the thrilling story of real men and women, and of their enthusiasm for the living faith by which they framed their lives. Part of their way of expressing this faith was in stone – in the rich heritage of churches and other features, which this book alerts us to in such an interesting and informative way. But our richest heritage is in what they were – and are; the people of yesterday, and the people of today in Cumbria, who are fired by this same living faith, and who have taken it up where the people of yesterday left off.

The past is all around us in Cumbria. Every morning when I look out of my kitchen window, it is through a gap in a three foot wall, which was once the ground floor of a peel tower built to keep out marauding Scots. And through the window I can see the village church, also fortified against the Scots, but built to mark one of the spots where St. Cuthbert's body rested on its journey south from over the fells in search of its final resting place. Men and women like Cuthbert were "giants" who stand out from the pages of history, but their prayer would certainly be that the Church of today would produce its own "giants" too. It is God who makes saints, of course – but there is plenty in this book to encourage us when it comes to the Church of today, and the signs of the Spirit's activity are all around us in Cumbria for those who have eyes to see. The past points us to the present, to the task that God has given his people in this northern corner of England today, and to the heritage that we in our turn must hand on to those who follow us. This book has been produced to mark the year of our 850th Anniversary celebrations. After them will come the 900th! What will people be writing about us and our part in the story, then?

† *George Hacker.*

Finding out More

A book like this can only scratch the surface. There are two ways of going deeper. First, go out and see for yourself. In the book, we have tried to point out some of the places where Christians of the past have left visible signs of their struggles and their hopes: from almost any point in the county, half an hour's drive will take you to at least five of them. Second, read on. There are reading lists for each Chapter, and here is a selection of works which span the whole period. Some are obtainable from the larger public libraries, some are in paperback at moderate prices.

On the history of Christianity, see J. R. H. Moorman, *A History of the Church in England* (Adam and Charles Black, 3rd edition, 1973), and Paul Johnson, *A History of Christianity* (Penguin, 1978).

For Cumbria, the first eight hundred years of the Diocese were ably recorded by Canon C. M. Lowther Bouch, *Prelates and People of the Lake Counties, 1133-1933* (Titus Wilson, 1948, and sadly out of print). See also the chapter by the Revd. James Wilson on "Ecclesiastical History" in the *Victorian History of the County of Cumberland*, Volume ii (1905, reprinted by Dawson 1968); H. L. Widdup, *Christianity in Cumbria* (Titus Wilson, 1981), and John Burgess, *A History of Cumbrian Methodism* (Titus Wilson, 1980).

On the physical remains of the past, refer to Sir Nikolaus Pevsner's volumes *Cumberland and Westmorland* (1967) and *North Lancashire* (1969), in the Pelican *Buildings of England* series.

The social history of the area is covered in C. M. L. Bouch and G. P. Jones, *A Short Economic and Social History of the Lake Counties 1500-1830* (Manchester University Press, 1961), and Roy Millward and Adrian Robinson, *The Lake District* (Eyre and Spottiswoode, 1970). Norman Nicholson's *The Lake District, An Anthology* (Penguin, 1981) is full of good things.

No delver into the past will get very far without referring to the *Transactions of the Cumberland and Westmorland Archaeological and Antiquarian Society* (old series 1866-1900, new series 1901-). There is hardly a church, a castle, or a monument that is not the subject of an article in these pages. To find them, refer to the indexes published for the years 1866-1900, 1901-1945, and 1946-1972, and to the useful, but not wholly accurate or complete, *Bibliography of the History and Topography of Cumberland and Westmorland* (1968, obtainable from the Record Office at Carlisle Castle).

The Royal Commission on Historical Monuments of Westmorland is a very useful book.

CHAPTER 1

There has been new thinking on the early history of our area, and many local traditions have been called into question, and new insights gained from archaeology. The reader should move warily! See especially Charles Thomas, *The Early Christian Archaeology of North Britain* (Oxford, 1971), Richard N. Bailey, *Viking Age*

Sculpture (Collins, 1980), and Alfred C. Smyth, *Scandinavian York and Dublin* (Templekieran Press, Dublin, 1975-79).

D. P. Kirkby's article "Strathclyde and Cumbria" in *CWAAS Transactions*, new series, lxii (1962) helps to sort out the confused political history.

The best general account of the church before 1066 is by Margaret Deanesly, *The Pre-Conquest Church in England* and *Sidelights on the Anglo-Saxon Church* (Adam and Charles Black, 1963 and 1962).

There is one contemporary historian who towers over all before and most after: the Venerable Bede (672/3-735), the Northumbrian who wrote *The Ecclesiastical History of the English Nation*, *The Life and Miracles of St. Cuthbert*, and *The Lives of the Abbots of Monkwearmouth and Jarrow*. The translations in the Everyman Series (1910, in print) and Penguin Classics (1955) can be read with pleasure by anyone today.

CHAPTER 2

For background on the Church History of the Middle Ages, start with J. C. Dickinson, *The Later Middle Ages* (Adam and Charles Black, 1979 – incidentally the work of a native of Cartmel), and Sir Richard Southern, *Western Church and Society in the Middle Ages* (Pelican, 1970), as well as Colin Platt, *Parish Churches of Medieval England* (Secker & Warburg, 1981).

Other works which the writer has found helpful are William A. Kapelle, *The Norman Conquest of the North* (Croom Helm, 1979), Professor Geoffrey Barrow's article "Northern Society in the Twelfth and Thirteenth Centuries" (*Northern History*, Volume iv, 1969), Rose, *The Labourer in the Vineyard* (Borthwick Papers No. 35, St. Anthony's Hall, York), and R. S. Ferguson, *Testamenta Karleolensia* (*CWAAS Extra Series*, 1893).

CHAPTER 3

There is an account of each religious house in Cumberland and Lancashire in the *Victoria County History*. All the monastic ruins are described in T. Clare, *Archaeological Sites of the Lake District*, with full illustrations (Morland Publishing, 1981), while Cartmel is favoured with J. C. Dickinson's *The Land of Cartmel: A History* (Titus Wilson, 1980).

On monastic background, see the attractive *English Abbeys and Priories* by Olive Cook and Edwin Smith, and then look into the standard works by Dom David Knowles, *The Monastic Order in England and The Religious Orders in England* (Cambridge University Press, 1940-1959). The end of Cartmel, Conishead and Furness is treated readably by Christopher Haigh, *The Last Days of the Lancashire Monasteries and the Pilgrimage of Grace* (Chetham Society, 1969) and *Reformation and Resistance in Tudor Lancashire* (Cambridge University Press, 1975).

CHAPTER 4

There are a number of histories of education; helpful is J. W. Anderson, *English Education 1789/1902* (CUP, 1930). Cornelius Nicholson, *Annals of Kendal 1862 ed* gives a complete run down on education in Kendal, and directories and local histories provide information throughout the 19th century.

Kenneth Harper, *The Story of the Lakeland Diocese 1933/66* is illuminating for modern trends.

CHAPTER 5

Most Nonconformist chapels have had their history written, normally as part of a centenary celebration, and these, along with parish church histories, can be found in county record offices, if not in the buildings themselves.

Every town, except Carlisle, has a satisfactory history of its denominations; for example, Daniel Hay on Whitehaven, John Marshall on Barrow, and J. F. Curwen and Cornelius Nicholson on Kendal.

R. S. Ferguson, *Early Cumberland and Westmorland Friends* and David Butler, *Quaker Meeting Houses of the Lake Counties* are outstanding contributions to the region's history. David Douglas wrote a *History of the Baptists of the North of England* in 1843, and, in this century, Whitley wrote *The Baptists of North West England* which explores the subject fully. *A History of Cumbrian Methodism* by John Burgess covers the whole of the Carlisle district, and the thesis upon which it is based gives as complete a list as possible of sources and publications regarding Methodism in the Diocese.

CHAPTER 6

J. D. Marshall and J. K. Walton, *The Lake Counties 1830 to the mid-20th century* (1981) takes on from when Bouch and Jones leave off.

The *Transactions of the CWAAS* contain a wealth of information, for instance, E. W. Hodge, *Stained Glass of the 19th Century and later in the Diocese of Carlisle*, lxxv, 1975, pp. 199/213. Owen Chadwick has written two weighty tomes on *The Victorian Church* (Adam and Charles Black) for the more persevering reader of Church history.

CHAPTER 7

Norman Nicholson, *The Lakers*, 1955 and *Portrait of the Lakes*, 1972. J. C. Pollock, *The Keswick Story*, 1964. E. W. Hodge, *Enjoying the Lakes*, 1957. H. D. Rawnsley, *Literary Associations of the English Lakes*, 1894, three volumes. H. A. L. Rice, *Lake Country Portraits*, 1967.

CHAPTERS 8 and 9.

Gerald Priestland's *Priestland's Progress*, 1981.

DIOCESE OF CARLISLE

850th Anniversary Prayer

"Father of all
We thank you for the past;
Strengthen our present;
And guide us in the future
In the power of Jesus Christ.   Amen."

Index of Place Names

Abbey Town, 24
Addingham, 3, 4, 29
Aldgate, 19
Alston, 37
Ambleside, 29, 41
Anthorn, 48
Appleby, 13, 18, 20, 28, 30, 40, 48
Arlecdon, 24, 40
Armathwaite, 20, 26
Arnside, 40
Askam, 38
Askham, 42
Aspatria, 2, 3, 11, 31

Bampton, 20, 29
Barrow-in-Furness, ii, 30, 32, 33, 37, 38, 40, 42, 43
Barton, 29
Beckermet, 4, 32, 40
Beetham, 29
Beverley, 28
Bewcastle, 3, 8, 20, 28
Bewley, 18
Bigrigg, 40
Birdoswald, 2
Blackford, 32
Blencow, 29
Bolton, 13, 14, 18
Boltongate, 17
Bootle, 12, 16, 20
Borrowdale, 20, 41
Bowness, 29, 41
Bradenstoke, 19
Brampton, 38, 42
Brantwood, 45
Bramwra, 17
Bridekirk, 14, 29, 43
Briggflatts, 35
Brigham, 4, 10, 40
Bristol, 48
Bromfield, 3, 29
Brotherilkeld, 25
Brough, 20, 28
Brougham, 1, 2;
Broughton, 29, 40, 43
Burgh-by-Sands, 17
Burneside, 32, 43
Burton, 29

Caldbeck, 3, 20, 29
Calder, 14, 20, 21, 22, 26
Calder Valley, 40
Calthwaite, 32
Cambridge, 29, 30
Camerton, 40
Carlisle, 1-6, 12, 17-22, 27-30, 32, 33, 36, 38, 40, 42, 43, 53, 55
Cartmel, 13, 17, 19, 21, 22, 26, 27, 29
Castle Sowerby, 3, 14
Chester, 13, 30
Chester-le-Street, 5
Citeaux, 19
Cleator, 38, 40
Cleator Moor, 38

Clifton, 14, 40
Cockermouth, 17, 28, 53
Cockersand, 20
Conishead, 13, 19, 21, 26
Coniston, 44, 45, 54
Copeland, 20
Corby, 33, 39
Corney, 16
Crosby Garrett, 29
Crosby Ravensworth, 32, 42
Cross Canonby, 10
Crosthwaite, Keswick, 3, 17, 32, 44
Cumdivock, 43

Dacre, 4, 10, 19, 28
Dalemain, 26
Dalston, 30, 40
Dalton, 13, 29, 38, 43, 53
Dean, 13, 29
Dearham, 10, 40
Dendron, 29
Dentdale, 35
Derwent, 5, 13, 21
Derwentwater, 5
Distington, 38, 40
Dodding Green, 33
Dronfield, 40
Dublin, 5
Dunmail Raise, 13
Durham, 5, 6, 9, 14

Eden Valley, 3, 21, 30
Edinburgh, 18
Egremont, 13, 40
Eskdale, 16, 24, 43, 44

Finsthwaite, 43
Flookburgh, 43
Frizington, 26
Furness, 16, 20-22, 25, 26, 28, 33, 35

Gamblesby, 43
Gilling, 22, 52
Gilsland, 9, 19-21
Gilswath, 20
Glasgow, 3, 12
Glassonby, 4
Gosforth, 6-9, 14, 35
Grange-in-Borrowdale, 20
Grange-over-Sands, 40
Grasmere, 41
Great Broughton, 38
Great Salkeld, 17, 38
Greystoke, 39, 53
Grinsdale, 3

Haverigg, 38
Haverthwaite, 53
Hawkshead, 20, 29, 35
Hawkshead Hill, 38
Heversham, 4, 6, 19, 28, 29
Hexham, 28
Holm Cultram, 20-22, 24-27, 31
Hutton-in-the-Forest, 17
Hutton Roof, 48

Ings, 29
Ireleth, 32

Irthington, 3
Irton, 6-8
Isle of Man, 6

Jarrow, 19

Kelsick, 29
Kendal, 4, 10, 12, 17, 18, 20, 28, 32, 33, 35, 37, 40, 42, 48, 53
Keswick, 29, 41, 44, 46, 48
Kirkbampton, 42
Kirkby-in-Furness, 10
Kirkby-Ireleth, 29
Kirkby Lonsdale, 10, 14, 18, 20, 29, 53
Kirkby Stephen, 4, 10, 20, 29, 38
Kirkland, 40
Kirkoswald, 20

Lakeside, 44
Lancaster, 16, 43
Lanercost, 9, 14, 15, 18, 19, 22, 23, 26, 42
Lazonby, 32
Lindisfarne, 5
Linstock, 18
Long Marton, 14
Longtown, 38, 40
Loweswater, 47
Lowther, 4, 10, 29, 30

Madras, 55
Manchester, 48
Maryport, 30, 38
Melrose, 20
Middleton, 43
Milburn, 16
Millom, 33, 38, 40
Monkwearmouth, 19
Moor Row, 38, 40
Moresby, 40
Morland, 9, 10
Mosser 32
Muncaster, 42
Mungrisdale, 3
Morecambe Bay, 2, 21

Natland, 32
Naworth, 39, 42
Netherby, 30, 39
Netherton, 53
Neville's Cross, 18
Newcastle, 42
Newlands, 43
Newton Arlosh, 17, 24, 52
Ninekirks, 2
Norham-on-Tweed, 6
Nostell, 12, 19
Nunnery, 20

Old Hutton, 29
Orton, 32
Ousby, 47
Oxford, 29, 30

Patterdale, 2
Penrith, 4, 18, 20, 28, 30, 47, 56
Penruddock, 43
Pentney, 19
Plumbland, 43
Ponsonby, 13, 42

Pooley Bridge, 43
Port Carlisle, 40
Preston Patrick, 2, 20

Ravenglass, 20, 38
Ravenstonedale, 20
Richmond, 13
Ripon, 56
Rose Castle, 18, 42
Rosley, 32
Rottington, 24
Rowrah, 40
Ruthwell, 4, 28
Rydal, 33, 54

St. Bees, 9, 10, 14, 16, 19, 22, 24, 25, 27, 29, 30, 40, 42
St. John's in the Vale, 54
Sandford, 20
Savigny, 19
Scaleby, 14
Scalthwaiterigg, 20
Scotby, 32
Seascale, 40
Seathwaite, 47
Seaton, 20, 26
Sebergham, 43
Selside, 32
Shap, 14, 20, 22, 24-27, 30, 37
Silloth, 38, 40, 43
Skinburness, 24
Skirwith, 32
Solway, 2, 3, 24, 40
Stainmore, 12, 29
Stainton, 32
Stavanger, 55
Staveley, 42
Strathclyde, 3, 9
Swarthmoor, 35, 38

Torver, 38, 43
Triermain, 9
Torpenhow, 14
Troutbeck, 29, 42
Tulketh, 19

Ulverston, 29, 30, 35
Urswick, 4, 29

Waberthwaite, 4
Wakefield, 12, 19
Walton, 10
Warcop, 20
Warwick, 42
Walton, 20
Welton, 43
Wetheral, 19, 22, 27
Whitbeck, 13
Whitby, 19
Whitehaven, 35, 37, 38, 40, 46, 53
Whithorn, 2
Wiggonby, 32
Wigton, 20, 30, 40
Windermere, 32, 41, 44, 53
Workington, 4, 5, 13, 39, 40
Wythburn, 42, 43

York, 12, 13, 19, 20, 22

Zululand, 55